# TAEKWON-DO KICKS

**Techniques, Strength & Flexibility**

White to Blue Belt

TAEKWON-DO
ITF
Sally Gleaves
VI
itf

**Sally Gleaves**

6th Degree ITF Taekwon-Do

# TAEKWON-DO KICKS

**Techniques, Strength & Flexibility**

White to Blue Belt

THE CROWOOD PRESS

Sally Greaves
VI
ITF TAE KWON DO 태권도

# Contents

ITF
태권도

# Introduction

Welcome to *Taekwon-Do Kicks*, a comprehensive guide designed to enhance your kicking abilities and elevate your performance in Taekwon-Do. In this book, we will delve into the intricacies of the kicking techniques that you'll need to master to achieve white to blue belts, providing step-by-step instructions, valuable insights, and exercises to help you improve your martial arts kicks, and prepare you to learn the more advanced techniques.

## WHY THIS BOOK MATTERS

As a coach and martial artist, one of the most frequent questions I hear is, 'How can I improve my kicks?' Kicking is at the heart of Taekwon-Do and many other martial arts, yet it can feel elusive for many students. They may know the basic movements, but struggle to achieve the power, speed and precision they aspire to. Beyond technique, I'm also regularly asked, 'How do I become more flexible?' These two questions – improving kicks and gaining flexibility – inspired me to create this book.

What many martial artists don't realise is that great kicking doesn't come solely from flexibility. While flexibility is important, effective kicking is the result of strengthening the body, improving mobility, and learning to move in a way that optimises power and balance. A kick is a full-body action that requires coordination, strength, balance, and mobility. It's about training your entire body to work in harmony, from your stance to your core engagement, to the snap and recovery of the kick itself.

This book is not just a collection of drills; it's a guide to understanding the *why* and *how* behind your kicks. By focusing on flexibility, strength, balance, mobility and biomechanics, I aim to help you build a more functional body capable of delivering powerful, precise and effective kicks. Whether you're looking to improve your sparring, your patterns or your overall physical health, this book will give you the tools to progress.

My goal is to provide a structured path to enhance kicking ability, not just through repetition but through understanding. Together, we'll work on building a stronger, more mobile and more resilient body, capable of delivering the kicks you've always wanted to achieve.

In short, this book is for everyone who has ever asked themselves, 'How can I kick better?'

## HOW TO USE THIS BOOK

To maximise the benefits of this book, it's essential to approach it with a structured and growth mindset. Begin by familiarising yourself with the theory of power in Chapter 1, as it provides the foundational principles that underpin effective kicking. From there, progress through each chapter systematically, as they cover the basics of Taekwon-Do and how to practise safely. In Part 2, focus on one kicking technique at a time, referring back to the appropriate chapters when you learn a kick at your classes.

As you delve into each kick chapter, start with the fundamental elements section to grasp the basic components of the kick and its variations. Follow along with the dynamic stretching warm-up routine to prepare your body for practice. Pay close attention to the correct technique section, where the biomechanical principles underlying the kick are explained in detail.

The incorrect technique section highlights common mistakes to avoid. You can also understand how to effectively utilise the kick in various contexts, whether it's sparring or self-defence.

Incorporate the basic strength, mobility and conditioning exercises into your training regimen to enhance your physical attributes. Dedicate time to static stretching for flexibility to improve your range of motion and prevent injuries.

Utilise the follow-along instructions and photos provided in each chapter to visualise and reinforce your understanding of each technique.

By following this structured approach, you'll gradually enhance your kicking abilities and overall performance in Taekwon-Do and unlock your full potential.

## MY TAEKWON-DO JOURNEY

My journey into Taekwon-Do was sparked by a tough experience with bullying during my school days. Seeking a solution to combat this challenge and boost my confidence, my parents found a local martial arts class; I found my way into the world of martial arts, and it soon became a lifelong passion.

Over the past 27 years, I have delved into various martial arts disciplines, starting with karate before transferring to Taekwon-Do. I took up kickboxing, MMA, and aikido alongside my Taekwon-Do. Under the guidance of many esteemed masters, I've progressed through the ranks, earning my 6th Dan in 2024.

Representing England on the international stage has been a source of immense pride for me. I've competed in numerous competitions, securing medals in patterns, sparring, and destruction. From receiving Coach of the Year at the Worcester Sports Awards to winning multiple World Championship medals, each accolade represents a milestone in my journey.

Beyond competing, I found my calling in instruction. After attaining my 1st Dan Black Belt, I pursued a professional qualification in Education, specialising in teaching Taekwon-Do. This marked a pivotal moment as I combined my passion for martial arts with formal education, shaping me into a dedicated instructor.

My commitment to education and inclusivity is reflected in my ongoing advocacy for women's equality and safety in Taekwon-Do. I am deeply involved in safeguarding and awareness initiatives, delivering presentations and workshops on topics such as sexual grooming and safety within the martial arts community.

As a leader in coach development in England, I focus on nurturing the next generation of martial arts instructors. From conducting workshops to delivering coaching qualifications, I am dedicated to raising coaching standards and supporting the growth of emerging talent. In addition, I am also a qualified personal trainer and gym instructor, ensuring that my sessions prioritise both physical and mental well-being. The array of qualifications under my belt include:

- Level 7 Certificate in Sports Coach Development
- PGCE (FE) Teaching – subject specialism in Martial Arts
- Level 2 Coaching Inclusive Martial Arts
- Level 2 Safeguarding Children and Vulnerable Adults
- Level 2 Exercise and Mental Health
- PREVENT
- First Aid Trained
- Mental Health First Aid Trained
- Enhanced DBS checked

All in all, I am equipped to provide a safe and enriching training environment.

My journey is adorned with numerous world titles, each representing the culmination of years of dedication and hard work, including:

- Gold – ITF Taekwon-Do World Championships 2020, 2021 and 2022
- Silver – Kickboxing Union World Championships 2013
- Bronze – Unified ITF Taekwon-Do World Championships 2013

Precision. Power. Control. A high front kick delivered with the ball of the foot, aimed directly to the opponent's face. This technique demands balance, flexibility and perfect timing. It's not just about height; it's about striking with accuracy and intent. Executed well, it can stop an opponent in their tracks.

VI

# PART 1

# ESSENTIAL BUILDING BLOCKS FOR GREAT KICKING TECHNIQUE

# 1 THE ESSENCE OF TAEKWON-DO POWER

In martial arts, power is not simply about brute force or physical strength. It's an intricate blend of power, technique, focus and understanding. Underpinning International Taekwon-Do Federation (ITF) Taekwon-Do, a Korean martial art renowned for its powerful kicks, lies the concept of the theory of power. This theory, elucidated by the founder, General Choi Hong Hi, is essential for practitioners to comprehend, as it forms the cornerstone of their training and practice.

## ORIGINS OF THE THEORY

To grasp the essence of Taekwon-Do power, we must delve into its origins. General Choi, drawing from his extensive knowledge of various martial arts, military strategy and scientific principles, formulated a comprehensive theory that encompasses both the physical and mental aspects of combat.

In ITF Taekwon-Do, the power behind Taekwon-Do techniques is achieved by utilising an individual's full potential through the precise application of techniques. Most people use only 10–20 per cent of their potential, but with proper training, anyone, regardless of size, age or gender, can reach their full capacity and execute powerful techniques. While training enhances physical fitness, true power comes from mastering reaction force, concentration, balance, breath control and speed rather than from extraordinary strength or stamina.

A textbook front kick, lifted with control, extended with purpose and executed using the ball of the foot. This technique showcases clean mechanics, sharp intent and solid posture. Whether used for sparring or self-defence, good form ensures speed, precision and impact exactly where it counts.

Applying the theory of power in Taekwon-Do through a turning kick board break. Reaction force, equilibrium, breath control and mass rotation are used to maximise speed and impact while maintaining precise foot positioning and hip rotation for optimal striking surface contact.

## ELEMENTS OF THE THEORY OF POWER

The theory of power in Taekwon-Do revolves around six fundamental elements:

- Mass
- Speed
- Reaction force
- Concentration
- Equilibrium
- Breath control

### Mass

Mass, or the body's weight, is the first essential element of power in Taekwon-Do. By understanding how to effectively utilise mass in motion, practitioners can greatly enhance the impact of their techniques. Proper weight distribution, balance and alignment are crucial to this process. When delivering a kick, such as a powerful turning or roundhouse kick, the practitioner must pivot on the supporting foot and transfer their body's mass into the striking leg. This transfer of weight significantly increases the force of the kick upon impact.

One key way to increase the body's mass in a kick is by turning the hip. Engaging the large abdominal muscles and rotating the hip in the same direction as the kicking leg adds momentum and effectively channels the body's weight into the strike. This hip rotation is critical for maximising impact.

Another method to increase power is the springing action of the knee joint. By slightly raising the hip at the start of the kick and lowering it at the moment of impact, body weight is dropped into the motion, further amplifying the force behind the kick. This combination of hip rotation and the springing action ensures that the body's full mass is directed into the kick, producing a powerful strike.

The principles of mass in Taekwon-Do are scientifically grounded, allowing practitioners to generate substantial power through the effective use of body weight. By mastering the techniques of weight transfer, balance and hip rotation, practitioners can deliver kicks that carry immense power and precision, maximising their effectiveness in combat.

### Speed

For effective kicking, speed is the most essential factor in generating power, especially when it comes to kicking techniques. Scientifically, force is a product of mass and acceleration, meaning that the faster a kick is executed, the more forceful and impactful it becomes. Speed transforms potential energy into kinetic energy, allowing practitioners to deliver powerful kicks that can break through an opponent's defences swiftly and efficiently.

Consider the example of a small stone thrown at high speed against glass – the glass shatters, demonstrating that even a small object can generate great force if accelerated rapidly. Similarly, in Taekwon-Do, the effectiveness of a kick relies not just on strength but on the speed at which it is delivered. A slow kick, no matter how strong, lacks the power to be effective. However, a fast, well-aimed kick can penetrate an opponent's defences and deliver a decisive blow.

Kicks such as a turning kick or side kick gain even more force when executed with speed and the correct trajectory. The principle of kinetic energy applies here as well; for example, a downward kick, like an axe kick, increases both weight and momentum during its descent, making it particularly destructive when the foot lands lower than the hip at the moment of impact.

Speed alone, however, is not enough. A fast kick must also be precise and controlled. A sloppy, rushed kick can leave the practitioner off-balance or vulnerable to counter-attacks. For instance, while a slow pass through a flame leaves it undisturbed, a controlled, fast kick can extinguish it.

Other elements, such as reaction force, breath control, balance and muscle relaxation, also play crucial roles in enhancing speed. These components, along with flexible and rhythmic movements, contribute to generating maximum power in kicking techniques. Through disciplined training and practice, Taekwon-Do practitioners can harness speed to deliver fast, powerful kicks that are both efficient and highly effective in combat.

Executing a reverse turning kick with a focus on counter-rotation as a reaction force. The kick demonstrates effective use of the theory of power through rotational mass, equilibrium and precise striking surface alignment, maximising both speed and impact through controlled hip and upper body movement.

## Reaction Force

Reaction force is a principle rooted in physics and essential to Taekwon-Do. According to Newton's Third Law, for every action there is an equal and opposite reaction. In Taekwon-Do, practitioners use this concept to increase the power of their techniques. By applying force against a surface – whether the ground during a kick or an opponent during a strike – an equal force is generated in the opposite direction, adding momentum and power to the technique. For example, when executing a punch, the practitioner not only drives the fist forwards but also pulls the opposite hand back to the hip, creating a reaction force that boosts the punch's impact.

Similarly, in kicking, the use of reaction force is crucial to generating power. For instance, when delivering a roundhouse or side kick, the practitioner can counter-rotate the arms, pulling them in the opposite direction of the kicking leg to increase the momentum and force of the kick. Additionally, the force exerted against the ground by the supporting leg during a kick generates a reaction force that transfers through the body, magnifying the power of the strike. The proper use of balance and body rotation, combined with this reaction force, allows practitioners to deliver kicks with greater velocity and impact.

In combat, reaction force becomes even more evident. As per Newton's Law, if an opponent rushes towards you with speed, the force of their momentum adds to the force of your kick. Even a well-placed kick with moderate power can become much more effective when it combines with the opponent's forward movement. This principle allows practitioners to strategically use their opponent's energy to enhance the effectiveness of their own kicks, creating a significant and sometimes unexpected impact.

This reaction force is not limited to the physical action of the limbs. The entire body contributes to the process, especially through the rotation of the hips and the stabilisation of the core. By engaging the large muscles in the abdomen and hips, the body channels additional momentum into the kick, making the strike more powerful. For example, during a spinning kick, the rotation of the body acts as a lever, increasing the velocity of the kicking leg and delivering a more powerful strike upon impact.

The principle of reaction force in Taekwon-Do is not just about generating power in punches but is equally essential for kicks. By using both the body's natural movements and the opponent's momentum, practitioners can deliver explosive, efficient, and highly effective kicks that maximise the force of each technique.

## Concentration

Power is maximised by focusing the impact force onto the smallest possible target area, increasing its effectiveness. Strikes are often concentrated on specific areas, such as the edge of the palm or the foot sword, to enhance impact. It is crucial not to unleash all your strength at once but to build it up gradually, concentrating the force at the moment of impact with the opponent's body. The shorter the time of concentration, the more powerful the strike, as maximum effort is directed onto the smallest target area at the exact moment of contact.

Concentration, or focus, is a critical element of power in Taekwon-Do. It not only involves physical precision but also mental clarity, visualisation and intent. Without concentration, physical strength alone is insufficient for effective techniques. By channelling mental energy and focusing on their target, practitioners ensure accuracy and maximum impact. Concentration also allows practitioners to stay calm under pressure, make quick decisions and adapt to rapidly changing situations in combat.

This principle works in two key ways. Firstly, it engages all the body's muscles, particularly the larger, slower muscles around the hips and abdomen, directing them with speed towards the striking tool at the right moment. Secondly, this power is concentrated on the opponent's vital spot. This is why the hips and abdomen are often engaged slightly before the hands or feet in any attack or defence, ensuring the full force is delivered at the point of impact.

Demonstrating a side kick on a BOSU ball, highlighting the importance of equilibrium in the theory of power. This exercise enhances balance, stability and core engagement, reinforcing control over mass and the ability to maintain a solid base of support while delivering maximum force through a precise striking surface.

## Equilibrium

Balance, or equilibrium, is critical for executing effective and powerful kicks. Whether attacking or defending, maintaining proper balance ensures precision, power and stability in movement. A well-balanced fighter can deliver more effective strikes, while one who loses their balance is vulnerable to being easily overpowered or toppled. The stance must be both stable and flexible, allowing for smooth transitions between offensive and defensive actions.

Equilibrium is divided into two types: dynamic and static stability. They are closely related, as the ability to generate maximum force depends on maintaining static stability during dynamic movements. For kicks to be truly effective, dynamic stability is essential, allowing the practitioner to move fluidly while keeping their body balanced.

To maintain proper equilibrium, the body's centre of gravity must be correctly positioned. When weight is distributed evenly between both legs, the centre of gravity should fall along a straight line between the legs. If the majority of weight is on one leg, the centre of gravity must be over that foot. Proper flexibility and a slight bend in the knees, known as 'knee spring', also help maintain balance, allowing for rapid attacks and swift recovery.

A key point for effective kicking is ensuring the standing foot remains grounded at the point of impact. Lifting the heel off the ground can compromise balance and reduce the power behind the kick. Keeping the standing foot stable allows for maximum power transfer and balance, enabling the practitioner to deliver strong, effective kicks while maintaining control throughout the movement.

### Breath Control

Breath control plays a vital role in executing effective kicks and maintaining overall performance. Controlled breathing not only impacts stamina and speed but also enhances the power behind each kick and helps the body withstand incoming strikes. Proper breath control can sharpen the delivery of a technique, ensuring that kicks are both powerful and precise.

When executing a kick, exhaling sharply at the moment of impact is essential. This sharp breath out tenses the abdomen, allowing for the concentration of maximum force into the kick. In contrast, stopping the breath during movement helps stabilise the body, enabling the kick to be delivered with greater power. Additionally, slow, controlled inhalation between movements helps prepare the body for the next strike, ensuring a smooth and efficient flow of energy.

It is critical to avoid inhaling during the execution of a strike or kick, as this can slow down movement and diminish the force of the technique. Proper breath timing enhances not only the effectiveness of the kick but also ensures that the practitioner remains fluid and balanced throughout the movement.

Breath control also plays a role in masking fatigue. Disguising breathing patterns can prevent an opponent from recognising signs of exhaustion, which could otherwise prompt them to press the attack. By maintaining steady, controlled breathing, a practitioner can manage their energy levels and maintain composure in combat, even under intense pressure.

In Taekwon-Do, each movement is paired with a corresponding breath, with the exception of some pattern *(tul)* motions. For effective kicks, this coordination between breath and movement is crucial, ensuring that each kick is delivered with precision, power, and efficiency.

## INTEGRATION OF ELEMENTS

The true power in Taekwon-Do lies in the seamless integration of its core elements: mass, speed, reaction force, and concentration, supported by equilibrium and breath control to maximise efficiency and effectiveness. Each element is vital on its own, but it is their combined synergy that unlocks the full potential of Taekwon-Do techniques. Mass provides the necessary force, speed amplifies it, reaction force channels it efficiently, and concentration ensures precision. When these elements work together in harmony, the practitioner is capable of delivering strikes and kicks with devastating power. Mastery of each individual aspect is important, but it is the synchronisation of all elements – body and mind moving as one – that truly defines the essence of Taekwon-Do. Something this author is working on consistently!

Achieving this level of performance requires more than just understanding the theory of power intellectually – it needs to be put into practice through consistent training and experience. As practitioners refine their skills, they begin to explore the deeper nuances of each element. They learn to apply their mass effectively, enhance their speed through agility, harness reaction force from the ground and their opponents, and sharpen their concentration to focus power at the precise moment of impact. The integration of these elements allows them to evolve beyond the mechanical execution of techniques, turning each movement into an expression of controlled force and power.

Through dedicated training, practitioners discover that Taekwon-Do is not only a physical practice but also a journey of personal growth. The harmony of mass, speed, reaction force and concentration reflects a balance between the physical and mental aspects of the martial art. This synergy transcends mere combat, shaping a martial artist who moves with purpose, intent, and precision. It is within this integration of elements that the true spirit of Taekwon-Do power is realised – an indomitable force that originates not just from the body, but from the unity of mind, technique, and energy.

Ultimately, Taekwon-Do is an art where power is cultivated, refined and channelled through disciplined training. By practising the integration of its elements, practitioners unlock the ability to deliver techniques that are not only effective in combat but also an expression of the deeper principles that define the martial art itself.

A high side kick delivered with the foot sword: sharp, controlled and perfectly aligned. This technique demands core strength, hip flexibility and precise chambering. It's a showcase of balance and intent, striking with maximum reach and power while maintaining full control through the line of the body.

# 2 TYPES OF KICK

Kicking techniques form the cornerstone of Taekwon-Do, showcasing the art's dynamic power, precision, and versatility. This chapter explores the various types of kick, covering both attacking and defensive techniques. Whether used to strike with force or to block and redirect an opponent's attack, kicks in Taekwon-Do rely on balance, speed and control. From the powerful thrust of an attacking kick to the subtle redirection of a defensive kick, each technique has its specific purpose and application. In this chapter, we will break down the principles behind these kicks, examine their variations, and provide insight into how they are effectively used in combat. Proficiency in both offensive and defensive kicking techniques is crucial for any practitioner, as they provide a well-rounded skill set that can be adapted to a wide range of fighting scenarios.

ITF Taekwon-Do kicks are classified into various types (*see* below), but they all follow common principles that are vital to their execution:

- **Maximum knee spring of the stationary leg** should always be employed to generate power and maintain balance.
- **Withdrawal of the kicking foot** must be immediate after the kick, with few exceptions, to prepare for the next movement and to prevent the leg from being grabbed by the opponent.
- **Body weight should shift** to the kicking leg at the moment of impact, and then return to the stationary leg immediately after.

Captured mid-motion, the turning kick extending with speed, balance, and precision. From chamber to execution, this technique flows with rotational power and sharp accuracy. A perfect example of timing, hip engagement and striking through the target with purpose.

Executing a powerful side kick, an offensive attacking technique known for its direct force and precision.

- **A strong stance** must be maintained with the stationary foot to ensure stability and balance throughout the kick.
- **Body alignment towards the target** is crucial. Once the kick is selected, the practitioner must adjust their body positioning to focus on the target effectively.
- **No pivoting of the stationary foot** should occur at the moment of impact to ensure maximum power transfer and maintain balance.
- **The heel of the stationary foot** must remain flat on the ground at the moment of impact to anchor the body and enhance the power of the kick.
- **The knee of the stationary leg** should be slightly bent to maintain balance at the point of impact, except in the case of a pressing kick.
- **The range and point of focus** for the kick must be calculated precisely, making adjustments based on the opponent's distance – whether they are too close or too far.
- **Most kicking movements begin with a backward motion** to gain momentum, increasing mass and velocity, except in some specific cases.

In addition to these fundamental principles, students of Taekwon-Do should also understand specific kicking terminology:

- **Double kick *(i-jung chagi)*** When the same type of kick is delivered twice in succession in the same direction by the same foot; can be executed against one or two opponents.
- **Triple kick *(samjung chagi)*** When the same type of kick is delivered three times in succession in the same direction by the same foot
- **Consecutive kick *(yonsok chagi)*** When two or more kicks are executed in succession by the same foot in different directions or with different tools
- **Combination kick *(honhap chagi)*** When both feet are used to deliver two or more kicks in succession; specific to flying kicks

In ITF Taekwon-Do, kicks are categorised into various types based on their techniques, purposes and applications. The following is an overview of the different types.

## ATTACKING KICKS

### Piercing Kicks

The piercing kick (*cha jirugi*) is a powerful and direct technique, similar in both theory and purpose to a punch. Its variants, the side piercing kick (*yopcha jirugi*), the back piercing kick (*dwitcha jirugi*) and the flying side piercing kick (*twimyo yopcha jirugi*), each target specific areas of the opponent's body, making it an effective tool in combat.

## Thrusting Kicks

Thrusting kicks (*cha tulgi*) in Taekwon-Do are designed to deliver powerful, direct strikes with an emphasis on forward-driving force. These kicks utilise the ball of the foot to focus the impact, making them effective for pushing through an opponent's defences. The main thrusting kicks are the side thrust kick (*yop cha tulgi*) and the flying side thrusting kick (*twimyo yopcha tulgi*).

## Smashing Kicks

The smashing kick (*cha busigi*) in Taekwon-Do is designed to deliver forceful and devastating strikes, similar in both purpose and method to hand strikes. These kicks focus on generating explosive impact to 'smash' through an opponent's defences. This family of kicks includes a number of variants, including the front snap kick, back snap kick, turning kick, twisting kick, reverse turning kick, reverse hooking kick, vertical kick, downward kick, pick-shape kick, straight kick, pressing kick and stamping kick.

## Pressing Kicks

The pressing kick (*noollo chagi*) is a controlled and forceful downward motion designed to press an opponent's limb or disrupt their balance. Unlike other kicks focused on sharp, impactful strikes, the pressing kick applies consistent downward pressure to specific areas of the opponent's body, making it a powerful tool in controlling an opponent or defending against certain attacks. The pressing kick comes in two main variations: inward pressing kick (*anuro noollo chagi*) and outward pressing kick (*bakuro noollo chagi*).

## Pushing Kicks

Pushing kicks (*milgi*) in Taekwon-Do are primarily used to push or drive an opponent backwards, rather than to cause immediate damage or injury. These kicks focus on utilising the body's weight and mass to shift the opponent off-balance or create space between them and the practitioner. Unlike piercing or thrusting kicks, pushing kicks lack the acceleration and power needed to penetrate the target, but they are highly effective for controlling an opponent's movement. The primary pushing kicks include the back pushing kick (*dwitcha milgi*), side pushing kick (*yopcha milgi*) and flying side pushing kick (*twimyo yopcha milgi*).

## Straight Kicks

The straight kick (*jigeau chagi*) is a direct, linear technique classified into front and back straight kicks, with the back heel as the primary attacking tool. Both legs remain straight during execution, with the front kick driving forward and the back kick delivered backwards to target an opponent. This kick is designed to create space, push the opponent back or counter attacks from behind. Its simplicity and precision make it effective for striking the opponent's torso or head; proper alignment and balance are crucial for maximising power and control.

## Sweeping Kicks

The sweeping kick (*suroh chagi*) is a technique designed to break an opponent's balance by targeting their outer ankle joint. It is typically executed using the side sole or back heel to sweep the opponent's leg, effectively destabilising them. This kick is useful for disrupting an opponent's stance and creating opportunities for follow-up attacks or takedowns. Its effectiveness lies in the precision and timing required to unbalance the opponent while maintaining control and balance.

## Consecutive Kicks

The consecutive kick (*yonsok chagi*) involves executing two or more kicks in succession using the same foot, targeting one or multiple opponents. These kicks can be performed in different directions or with different tools, and can follow either offensive or defensive moves. The key to effective consecutive kicking lies in maintaining balance on the stationary foot, allowing the kicking foot to continue without touching the ground. Various combinations of kicks can be used, such as a front snap kick followed by a side rising kick, or a reverse hooking kick followed by a side piercing kick. This technique can also be classified as a double or triple kick depending on the number of consecutive kicks. The flying consecutive kick (*twimyo yonsok chagi*) follows the same principles but is executed in mid-air, allowing for combinations such as crescent and side kicks or front and twisting kicks.

### Flying Kicks

The flying kick (*twimyo chagi*) is one of the most distinctive and dynamic techniques in Taekwon-Do, unparalleled in both variety and execution when compared to other martial arts. While some may argue that flying kicks are impractical or leave the practitioner vulnerable, experienced Taekwon-Do practitioners can attest that a well-executed flying kick delivered with speed is both powerful and surprising, often catching opponents off guard.

A student who becomes proficient with the flying kick can spring into the air and perform multiple kicks from a stationary position, even without taking an additional step. The advantages of flying kicks are numerous: they improve balance, develop coordination, strengthen muscles and refine timing and focus. Additionally, flying kicks are highly effective for attacking high targets, leaping over obstacles or attacks, and closing distance quickly.

## DEFENSIVE KICKS

In ITF Taekwon-Do, defence techniques play a crucial role in maintaining balance and control during combat. While hand techniques are commonly associated with blocking and dodging, the feet

Demonstrating a flying side kick, an advanced Taekwon-Do technique that showcases the application of power through elevation and distance.

provide a versatile and powerful alternative for defensive manoeuvres. Good footwork not only enhances the practitioner's ability to block attacks but also allows for greater freedom of movement and the ability to swiftly counter-attack. Techniques such as the rising kick, crescent kick, waving kick, checking kick and hooking kick demonstrate the effectiveness of footwork in defence, utilising precise movements to block or redirect an opponent's strike while maintaining balance and readiness for further action. These kicks, fundamental to the art of Taekwon-Do, showcase the dynamic range of defence available to practitioners, highlighting the importance of agility, control, and precision in responding to an opponent's attack.

## Rising Kick

The rising kick (*cha olligi*) consists of two variations: front rising kick (*apcha olligi*) and side rising kick (*yopcha olligi*). These techniques are primarily used to block attacks aimed at the middle or upper sections of the body by deflecting the opponent's punch or kick in an upward arc. The rising kick is also a key exercise for muscle development.

- **Front rising kick** uses the ball of the foot to spring up the opponent's fist or kick by targeting the under forearm or inner tibia. The knee of the kicking leg should remain only slightly bent to maintain form and effectiveness.
- **Side rising kick** employs the foot sword to spring up an opponent's attacking hand or foot. The body should be in a half-facing position at the start of the kick for optimal balance and control.
- Both kicks are often practised in walking, sitting, and diagonal stances to improve muscle strength.

## Crescent Kick

The crescent kick (*bandal chagi*) is an arcing motion used to block attacks coming from the side or at mid to high levels. The kick sweeps in an inward or outward arc, effectively deflecting the opponent's strike away from the practitioner's body. This kick requires precision in its arc to ensure the opponent's strike is redirected without causing harm.

## Waving Kick

The waving kick (*doro chagi*) is a defensive technique where the leg moves in a sweeping, wave-like motion to block or redirect an opponent's attack. This kick is typically used to handle attacks directed at the lower or middle sections of the body. The wave motion allows for a soft redirection of power, guiding the opponent's strike away from its intended target without necessarily causing a hard block.

## Checking Kick

The checking kick (*cha munchugi*) is used to interrupt or stop an opponent's attack by pushing or 'checking' the attacking limb. It can be applied to stop an opponent's advancing foot or arm before it makes contact. This kick is effective in halting the opponent's momentum while maintaining the practitioner's balance and positioning for a counter-attack.

## Hooking Kick

The hooking kick (*golcho chagi*) is a versatile blocking technique where the foot hooks around the opponent's limb to redirect their attack. This kick is particularly useful for catching and deflecting incoming strikes from the side. The hooking motion is quick and fluid, ensuring that the opponent's attack is neutralised without disrupting the practitioner's stance or balance.

Each technique, whether offensive or defensive, plays a critical role in a practitioner's skill set, and understanding their proper execution and application is essential for effective use. This book focuses on foundational and widely applied kicking techniques, while more advanced and specialised kicks will be explored in volume 2. The upcoming chapters will cover the principles, variations, and strategies behind the kicks included in this book, equipping you with the tools to fully integrate them into your Taekwon-Do practice.

The front kick is classified as a smashing kick in Taekwon-Do – driving upward with force, using the ball of the foot to strike through the target. It's a powerful, direct technique that combines speed, accuracy and impact, ideal for breaking the opponent's guard or disrupting forward motion.

# 3 KICKING BASICS

Kicking is one of the most distinctive and essential elements of ITF Taekwon-Do, embodying both the art's aesthetic appeal and its combative effectiveness. Understanding the basics of kicking is crucial for practitioners at all levels, as it forms the foundation for advanced techniques and applications. This chapter explores the core principles, biomechanics, steps of performing a kick, and training methodologies that underpin the kicking techniques in ITF Taekwon-Do.

## CORE PRINCIPLES OF KICKING

The execution of effective kicks in ITF Taekwon-Do is governed by several fundamental principles:

- **Balance and stability** Maintaining balance is crucial during the execution of kicks. This involves a stable stance, proper weight distribution and core strength to prevent being off-balanced by the opponent.
- **Speed and power** Kicks must be delivered with both speed and power. This combination is achieved through correct muscle engagement, proper technique and explosive movements.
- **Accuracy and precision** Effective kicking targets specific vital points on the opponent's body. Precision ensures that the kick lands accurately, maximising its impact while minimising the risk of counter-attacks.

Training kicks with added resistance builds true functional power. Holding a kettlebell while kicking challenges balance, core strength and control – developing the stability needed to deliver powerful, grounded techniques under pressure. Strength meets precision in every rep.

- **Flexibility and range of motion** Flexibility in the hips, legs and lower back enhances the range of motion, allowing for higher and more versatile kicks. Regular stretching and flexibility exercises are integral to developing these attributes.
- **Timing and rhythm** Understanding the timing and rhythm of an attack and defence sequence is essential. Getting it right allows the practitioner to execute kicks at the optimal moment for maximum effectiveness.

## BIOMECHANICS OF KICKING

Understanding the biomechanics of kicking in ITF Taekwon-Do is essential for improving technique and performance. Biomechanics involves the study of the mechanical laws relating to the movement or structure of living organisms. Below are the key biomechanical aspects involved in Taekwon-Do kicks:

- **Kinetic chain** The concept refers to how different body parts and joints work together to produce movement. A well-executed kick involves a coordinated effort from the feet, legs, hips, torso and even the arms. The power generated from the ground travels through this kinetic chain, culminating in the striking foot.
- **Joint mechanics** The mechanics and mobility of the joints, especially the hip, knee and ankle, play a critical role in kicking. Proper joint alignment and movement ensure the efficient transfer of energy and reduce the risk of injury. For example, the hip joint needs to allow for the wide range of motion that is essential for high and powerful kicks.
- **Muscle activation** Different kicks require the activation of various muscle groups. Understanding which muscles are involved helps in targeting strength and conditioning exercises. The primary muscles involved in kicking include the quadriceps, hamstrings, glutes, hip flexors and core muscles.
- **Centre of mass** The centre of mass (COM) is crucial for maintaining balance and stability during kicks. Effective kicking involves managing the COM to ensure that the practitioner remains balanced while generating force. This often involves a slight shift or adjustment in body position.
- **Force production** Generating force for a kick involves both muscular strength and the elastic properties of muscles and tendons. The stretch-shortening cycle (SSC) is a key concept, where muscles are rapidly stretched before contracting to produce a more powerful movement.
- **Angular momentum** The rotation of the body, particularly in kicks like the turning kick, involves the concept of angular momentum. Properly managing rotational forces to achieve an optimal trajectory of the kick can increase the speed and impact of the kick. This involves not only the kicking leg but also the coordinated movement of the arms and torso.

## STEPS OF PERFORMING A KICK: CHAMBERING, EXTENSION, RECHAMBERING

Executing a kick in ITF Taekwon-Do involves a series of well-coordinated steps, which ensure that the kick is delivered with maximum efficiency, power and accuracy. The three primary steps are chambering, extension and rechambering (CER):

### Chambering

Chambering (C) is the initial phase of the kick, where the knee of the kicking leg is lifted and bent towards the chest. This position allows for the build-up of potential energy that will be converted into kinetic energy during the extension phase.

**Chambering (C)** Chambering is the first phase of a kick, where the knee of the kicking leg lifts towards the chest, storing potential energy. Key elements include balancing on the supporting leg, keeping the torso upright, aligning the hips, and positioning the arms for balance, counter-rotation and defence. Proper chambering ensures a straight, powerful kick to the target.

**Extension (E)** The extension phase releases the stored energy from chambering, driving the kicking leg towards the target. Power is generated through a swift, controlled movement with the correct striking surface – ball of the foot, heel or instep – depending on the kick. Hip rotation adds power and reach, ensuring accuracy and impact upon contact.

**Rechambering (R)** Rechambering is the process of retracting the kicking leg back to the chambered position after striking. It maintains balance, prevents the leg from being caught and prepares for follow-up moves like another kick, block or retreat. Proper rechambering controls momentum, allowing the practitioner to regain a stable stance and remain ready for further action.

Key aspects of chambering include maintaining balance on the supporting leg, ensuring the torso remains upright, and positioning the arms to aid balance and prepare for counter-rotation and potential counter-attacks.

Proper chambering also involves aligning the hips and torso to ensure that the kick can be delivered in a straight line towards the target.

## Extension

During the extension (E) phase, the kicking leg is rapidly extended towards the target. This is where the power of the kick is generated, as the stored energy from the chambering phase is released.

The extension should be swift and controlled, with the foot aimed accurately at the target. The type of kick determines the striking surface, whether it be the ball of the foot, the heel or the instep.

The hips play a crucial role in this phase, providing additional power and reach by rotating and driving the leg forward.

## Rechambering

Rechambering (R) involves retracting the kicking leg back to the chambered position after striking the target. This step is crucial for maintaining balance and preparing for subsequent movements, whether it be another kick, a block or a retreat.

Proper rechambering prevents the leg from being caught by the opponent and helps in regaining a stable stance.

The key striking and blocking areas of the foot used in Taekwon-Do kicks and defensive techniques. The ball of the foot is commonly used for powerful, precise strikes in kicks like the front kick. The back sole and back heel are effective striking tools in techniques such as the back kick and reverse hooking kick. The inner sole and side sole can be used for blocking or sweeping motions, while the toes must be properly aligned or flexed to avoid injury during kicks like the front snap kick. Proper foot positioning is essential to maximise impact and minimise injury risk during strikes and blocks.

This phase also aids in controlling the momentum of the kick, ensuring that the practitioner remains balanced and ready for further action.

## TRAINING METHODOLOGIES

Training to perform the kicks in ITF Taekwon-Do involves a blend of various exercises and drills:

- **Basic drills** These involve repetitive practice of each kick to develop 'muscle memory' (although strictly it's your nervous system that retains motor patterns and not your muscles), technique and endurance. Practitioners often perform kicks in the air or on pads and shields.
- **Flexibility exercises** Regular stretching routines are essential to improve flexibility. Dynamic stretches, static stretches and partner-assisted stretches all contribute to greater kicking range and efficiency.
- **Strength and conditioning** Strong legs and core muscles are crucial for powerful kicks. Exercises such as squats, lunges and plyometrics help build the necessary strength and explosiveness.
- **Target training** Kicking targets such as pads, bags and shields helps improve accuracy and power. They provide resistance and feedback, allowing practitioners to refine their technique.
- **Sparring and application** Applying kicks in sparring sessions helps practitioners understand the timing, distance and effectiveness of each technique. It also helps in developing reflexes and adaptability in a dynamic environment.

## SECTIONS VS HEIGHTS

In ITF Taekwon-Do, the distinctions between sections and heights are fundamental for executing techniques accurately. These classifications help practitioners target specific areas of the body effectively, ensuring precise and impactful movements.

### Sections

The high section (*nopunde bubun*) targets areas above the opponent's neck. Techniques in this section include high kicks, high punches, and strikes aimed at the head or neck. These moves are often intended to deliver knockout blows or to disorientate the opponent.

The body is divided into three target sections in Taekwon-Do: the high section *(nopunde bubun)* targets the head and neck, aiming to disorientate or deliver knockout blows. The middle section *(kaunde bubun)* focuses on the torso, striking vital areas like the solar plexus to cause significant impact. The low section *(najunde bubun)* targets below the navel to destabilise the opponent and limit their mobility.

The middle section (*kaunde bubun*) focuses on the area between the opponent's shoulders and navel. Techniques used here include middle punches, blocks, and kicks targeting the torso. The purpose is to cause significant impact by hitting vital organs and the solar plexus.

The low section (*najunde bubun*) targets areas below the opponent's navel. Techniques in this section involve low kicks, low punches, and blocks aimed at the lower part of the body. These moves are designed to destabilise the opponent and limit their mobility.

A well-executed nopunde (high section) kick – controlled, precise, and delivered at eye level. This technique showcases flexibility, balance and accuracy, targeting the opponent's head with sharp intent while maintaining strong posture and form.

## Heights

The high (*nopunde*) height involves executing techniques at the attacker's eye level. This level requires flexibility and balance, especially for high kicks.

The middle (*kaunde*) height pertains to techniques executed at the attacker's shoulder level, and is especially important for those competing in ITF Patterns. This height offers a balance between power and speed, making it a versatile range for both attacks and defences.

The low (*najunde*) height involves techniques aimed at the attacker's navel level. This height is effective for targeting the lower body and vulnerable points such as the knees and shins.

The kicks of ITF Taekwon-Do are a blend of artistry and martial skill, requiring diligent practice and a thorough understanding of fundamental principles. By acquiring the basics – balance, speed, accuracy, flexibility and timing – practitioners can perform a wide array of kicks with precision and power. A solid grasp of the biomechanics involved in kicking further enhances a practitioner's ability to execute techniques efficiently and effectively. The structured approach of chambering, extension and rechambering ensures that kicks are delivered with maximum effectiveness and control. Training methodologies that encompass drills, flexibility exercises, strength conditioning and practical application ensure that students develop the necessary skills to execute kicks effectively. As such, the kicking techniques in ITF Taekwon-Do not only define the martial art's unique character but also empower practitioners with formidable tools for self-defence and competition.

At the same time, understanding the differences between sections and heights enhances the effectiveness and control of techniques in ITF Taekwon-Do. Accurate targeting of sections ensures effective strikes and blocks, while the strategic use of different sections and heights can be tactically advantageous in sparring and self-defence. Through training, practitioners develop the strength, speed and accuracy necessary for executing techniques at each section and height, thereby improving their overall martial arts proficiency.

A powerful thrusting kick delivered with the ball of the foot, targeting the opponent's solar plexus. This technique drives forward with intent, using body weight and precision to penetrate defences and disrupt breathing – a perfect blend of control, accuracy and impact.

# 4 HIPS DON'T LIE

The tilt of the pelvis plays a significant role in Taekwon-Do, influencing the efficiency, power and accuracy of kicks. Pelvic tilt refers to the orientation of the pelvis in relation to the spine and legs, and it can be classified primarily into three types: anterior pelvic tilt (APT), posterior pelvic tilt (PPT) and neutral pelvic tilt (NPT).

A high twist kick in motion – hips fully opened to allow the technique to extend with height, precision and control. This dynamic movement demands flexibility and timing, with the rotation of the hip key to unlocking reach and power through the strike.

## ANTERIOR PELVIC TILT

An anterior pelvic tilt (APT) occurs when the front of the pelvis drops and the back of the pelvis rises. This position is characterised by an exaggerated arch in the lower back.

### Impact on Muscles

- **Hip flexors** Shortened and overactive
- **Hamstrings** Lengthened and under tension
- **Lower back** (**erector spinae**) Tightened and overactive
- **Abdominals** Lengthened and weakened.

### Impact on Kicking

*Lateral Kicks (eg Side Kick)*

- **Increased hip flexor activation** The shortened hip flexors engage more easily, facilitating the sideways lift for side kicks.

Anterior pelvic tilt (APT), where the pelvis tilts forward, creating an exaggerated lumbar curve and arching the lower back. This posture is commonly identified by the downward tilt of the front pelvis and the upward tilt at the back. It highlights poor pelvic alignment, which can impact balance, reduce kicking efficiency and increase strain on the lower back and hip flexors.

- **Enhanced range of motion** Greater external rotation of the hip aids a more fluid and powerful extension.
- **Stability and balance** The lower back and core work to maintain balance, which is crucial for precise and controlled kicks.

*Round Kicks (eg Turning Kick)*

- **Hip rotation** The active hip flexors improve hip rotation, enhancing kick speed and power.
- **Alignment issues** The exaggerated lumbar curve can cause misalignment, reducing accuracy.

*Linear Kicks (eg Front Snap Kick)*

- **Flexibility in extension** Active hip flexors aid in higher leg lifts, benefiting front snap kicks.
- **Lower back stress** Increased lumbar curve stress can lead to discomfort or injury during high kicks.

## POSTERIOR PELVIC TILT

A posterior pelvic tilt (PPT) occurs when the front of the pelvis rises and the back of the pelvis drops, flattening the lower back.

### Impact on Muscles

- **Hip flexors** Lengthened and less active
- **Hamstrings** Shortened and overactive
- **Lower back** (**erector spinae**) Lengthened and weakened
- **Abdominals** Tightened and overactive

### Impact on Kicking

*Lateral Kicks (eg Side Kick)*

- **Reduced external rotation** Limited hip external rotation restricts the range of motion for side kicks.
- **Balance issues** A disrupted centre of gravity can affect balance and stability during complex kicks.

*Round Kicks (eg Turning Kick)*

- **Core engagement** Stronger abdominal engagement aids in maintaining a solid core during kicks.
- **Limited hip rotation** Reduced hip flexor activity can limit hip rotation, affecting power and speed.

*Linear Kicks (eg Front Snap Kick)*

- **Enhanced hip extension** This facilitates greater hip extension, aiding in driving the leg forward.
- **Lower back protection Reduced** lumbar stress decreases lower back pain risk during repetitive kicks.

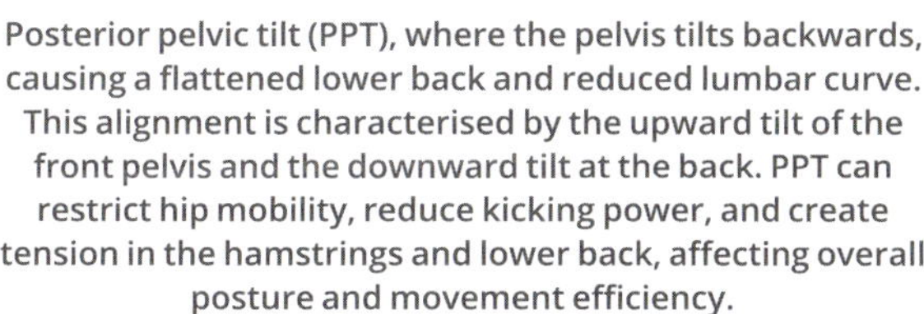
Posterior pelvic tilt (PPT), where the pelvis tilts backwards, causing a flattened lower back and reduced lumbar curve. This alignment is characterised by the upward tilt of the front pelvis and the downward tilt at the back. PPT can restrict hip mobility, reduce kicking power, and create tension in the hamstrings and lower back, affecting overall posture and movement efficiency.

Neutral pelvic tilt, where the pelvis is aligned in a balanced position, maintaining the natural curve of the lower back. In this position, the front and back of the pelvis are level, ensuring optimal posture, stability and movement efficiency. Neutral pelvic alignment allows for better core engagement, improved balance and more effective power transfer during kicking techniques.

## NEUTRAL PELVIC TILT

A neutral pelvic tilt (NPT) is when the pelvis is aligned so that the hip bones are level and there is a natural curve in the lower back without exaggeration.

### Impact on Muscles

- **Hip flexors** Balanced and functioning efficiently
- **Hamstrings** Neither overactive nor under tension
- **Lower back (erector spinae)** Maintains natural curve, balanced
- **Abdominals** Balanced and supporting the spine effectively

### Impact on Kicking

*Lateral Kicks (eg Side Kick)*

- **Optimal range of motion** A balanced hip range of motion allows optimal angles for side kicks.
- **Stability and control** Enhanced stability and control deliver precise and powerful kicks.

*Round Kicks (eg Turning Kick)*

- **Balanced hip rotation** Efficient hip rotation enhances power and accuracy.
- **Core and lower back synergy** Effective core and lower back collaboration supports high-speed kicks.

*Linear Kicks (eg Front Snap Kick)*

- **Efficient hip flexion and extension** Facilitates natural hip movement for fluid front snap kicks.
- **Lower back health** A neutral pelvic tilt maintains lumbar health, reducing injury risk.

## GENERAL CONSIDERATIONS

Both anterior and posterior pelvic tilts have their pros and cons in the context of Taekwon-Do kicks. The following are some key considerations:

- **Flexibility and strength balance** Ensuring a balance between flexibility and strength in the hip flexors, hamstrings and core muscles can mitigate the disadvantages of both pelvic tilts. Regular stretching and strengthening exercises are essential.
- **Posture awareness** Being aware of one's pelvic tilt and making necessary adjustments can improve kicking performance. For instance, consciously tilting the pelvis slightly anteriorly or posteriorly, depending on the kick, can enhance execution.
- **Technique training** Proper technique training under the guidance of a skilled instructor can help in optimising the use of pelvic tilt during kicks, ensuring that the advantages are maximised and the risks minimised.

### Be Kind to Yourself

It is important to understand that if your hip setup is limiting your kicks, it is not your fault. Everyone's body is different, and structural variations can significantly impact physical capabilities. Be kind to yourself and patient as you work on improving your kicks.

### Seeking Professional Help

Your Taekwon-Do instructor might not have the specialised knowledge to address issues related to pelvic tilt. If you are struggling with your kicks despite consistent practice and proper technique training, it may be worthwhile to consult a physiotherapist. A physiotherapist can assess your hips and pelvic alignment, providing tailored exercises and adjustments to help you overcome these limitations and improve your performance in Taekwon-Do.

A precise waving kick demonstrated with the hip in full external rotation.

# 5 INTRODUCTION TO STRETCHING, MOBILITY AND FLEXIBILITY

Before diving into the specifics of stretching techniques, it's essential to understand the distinction between mobility and flexibility, as both play critical roles in Taekwon-Do performance and injury prevention.

**Flexibility** refers to the range of motion of a muscle or joint, achieved by elongating the muscle through various stretches. It is largely influenced by the muscle's length and the elasticity of the surrounding connective tissues. In the context of Taekwon-Do, greater flexibility allows for a wider range of motion in kicks and techniques, enhancing performance and reducing the likelihood of muscle strains and tears.

Static flexibility in a seated side split position. This stretch targets the adductors, hamstrings and hip flexors, improving range of motion and overall flexibility. Holding a static stretch like this helps lengthen muscles and connective tissues, enhancing kicking height, control and injury prevention. Proper alignment and controlled breathing are essential to maximise the effectiveness of this stretch.

Delivering a high kick while standing on an unstable platform – a true test of stability, flexibility, mobility and balance. This level of control under challenging conditions reflects deep body awareness and refined technique, proving that power means nothing without precision and poise.

**Mobility**, on the other hand, encompasses not only the flexibility of muscles but also the ability of the joints to move freely through their full range of motion. It combines flexibility with strength, stability and control. Good mobility ensures that the joints can move effectively and safely while performing dynamic actions like high kicks or rapid changes in direction. While flexibility focuses on the muscle's ability to stretch, mobility includes how well the muscles and joints work together to perform movements smoothly and without restriction.

## KICK MOBILITY

Kick mobility refers to the combination of flexibility, strength and control required to execute kicks effectively and safely. It involves not only having the range of motion needed to perform a kick but also the strength and stability to control the movement throughout its execution.

### Key Components of Kick Mobility

- **Flexibility** is crucial for achieving a full range of motion in the leg and hip joints. Adequate flexibility allows you to lift your leg higher and perform kicks with greater ease and efficiency. For example, high kicks, such as head kicks, require significant flexibility in the hamstrings, quadriceps and hip flexors.
- **Strength** is essential to maintain control over the leg during the kick. It includes the power of the muscles involved in the kicking motion, such as the quadriceps, hamstrings, hip flexors and core muscles. Strong muscles help in executing powerful kicks and also in stabilising the body during the kick.
- **Control** is the ability to manage the movement of the leg and maintain proper technique throughout the kick. It includes balance, coordination and the capacity to adjust the kick mid-motion. Good control helps in accurately targeting and delivering the kick effectively while reducing the risk of injury.
- **Stability** refers to the ability to maintain a strong and balanced posture during and after the kick. Proper balance ensures that the practitioner remains in control and can recover quickly from the kicking motion, which is important for both defensive and offensive techniques.

### Enhancing Kick Mobility

- **Stretching** Incorporating a variety of stretching techniques – such as dynamic, static and PNF stretching – can improve flexibility, which is a critical aspect of kick mobility. Regular stretching helps maintain and enhance the range of motion in the hips and legs.
- **Strength training** Strengthening the muscles involved in kicking, including the quadriceps, hamstrings, glutes, and core, improves the power and control of the kick. Exercises like leg lifts, squats, and lunges can build strength and endurance.

- **Drills and technique practice** Practising kicks with proper technique and incorporating drills that focus on balance and control can improve kick mobility. Techniques such as slow-motion kicking and balance exercises help enhance both control and stability.
- **Mobility exercises** Specific exercises that focus on joint mobility and range of motion, such as hip circles and leg swings, can further enhance kick mobility. These exercises help improve the ability of the joints to move freely and efficiently.

By focusing on these components and incorporating targeted exercises into your training routine, you can improve your kick mobility, leading to more effective and controlled kicks in Taekwon-Do.

## IMPROVING MOBILITY

Improving mobility is essential for enhancing your range of motion, reducing the risk of injury, and boosting overall physical performance. It involves various practices and techniques that can be integrated into your routine to achieve better flexibility and joint function.

A front leg raise, a dynamic stretch that enhances flexibility, balance and kicking height. This stretch targets the hamstrings and hip flexors, warming up the muscles by moving through a controlled range of motion. Dynamic stretches like the front leg raise are essential for preparing the body for explosive movements, improving overall mobility and reducing injury risk.

### Dynamic Stretching

This is a key component in enhancing mobility, especially as part of your warm-up routine. It involves moving parts of your body through their full range of motion in a controlled manner. For example, performing leg swings can help loosen up your hips and hamstrings, while arm circles warm up your shoulders and upper back. Additionally, hip circles, where you rotate your hips in both directions, can improve hip mobility.

### Static Stretching

This important technique for improving flexibility and maintaining range of motion involves holding a stretch for a prolonged period, typically 20–30 seconds. Common static stretches include the hamstring stretch, where you sit with your legs extended and reach toward your toes, and the hip flexor stretch, which involves stepping one foot forward into a lunge position and pushing your hips forward. Shoulder stretches, where you bring one arm across your body and use the opposite arm to pull it closer, are also beneficial.

Using a foam roller to enhance flexibility and relieve muscle tension. Rolling forward with the foam roller targets the shoulders, back and lats, promoting an increased range of motion and reducing stiffness. Foam rolling aids in muscle recovery by improving blood flow and releasing tight fascia, making it an essential tool for martial artists to optimise performance and prevent injury.

## Foam Rolling

More scientifically known as self-myofascial release, this helps release muscle tightness and improve blood flow. By using a foam roller, you can apply pressure to specific muscle groups, such as the quadriceps, hamstrings or IT band. This technique aids in relieving muscle soreness and improving overall muscle function.

## Mobility Exercises

These focus specifically on enhancing joint mobility and muscle flexibility. Exercises like the 90/90 stretch, where you sit with one leg in front and the other behind, help stretch the hip flexors. Thoracic rotations, performed while sitting or standing with arms extended in front, improve upper back mobility. Ankle mobility exercises, such as ankle circles or knee-to-wall stretches, enhance the range of motion in your ankles.

## Other Exercises

Building strength in stabilising muscles is also crucial for supporting better joint mobility and control. Core strengthening exercises, such as planks and side planks, build stability. Balance exercises, like using balance boards or performing single-leg stands, further enhance balance and control.

Maintaining proper posture supports optimal joint alignment and movement. Being aware of your posture while sitting, standing and moving is essential. Postural exercises that strengthen the muscles supporting good posture, such as rows and shoulder blade squeezes, can contribute to better mobility.

Warming up and cooling down properly are integral to any training routine. Start with a dynamic warm-up to increase blood flow and prepare your muscles and joints for activity. Finish with a cool-down session that includes static stretching to relax your muscles and maintain flexibility.

Improving mobility requires consistent effort and integration of these practices into your regular training routine. By focusing on dynamic stretching, static stretching, foam rolling, mobility exercises, strength training and proper posture, you can enhance your mobility, improve overall performance, and reduce the risk of injury.

## THE ROLE OF STRETCHING IN TAEKWON-DO

Effective stretching is fundamental in Taekwon-Do for achieving powerful kicks and preventing injuries. Research has consistently shown that improved flexibility enhances athletic performance and lowers the risk of injuries. A well-rounded stretching regimen supports better kick execution by increasing range of motion, power and precision, while also reducing the chances of strains and tears.

### Dynamic Stretching

Dynamic stretching is a valuable warm-up technique that prepares the body for intense physical activity. Unlike static stretching, which involves holding stretches, dynamic stretching involves controlled, smooth movements that mimic the activity to come. Research indicates that dynamic stretching increases muscle temperature, blood flow, and neuromuscular function, which can lead to improved performance. For Taekwon-Do practitioners, dynamic stretching exercises like leg swings, high knees and hip circles enhance coordination and efficiency in kicking, making them an essential component of pre-training routines.

### Static Stretching

Static stretching involves holding a stretch for an extended period to increase muscle length and joint range of motion. Studies have shown that static stretching can effectively reduce muscle stiffness and improve overall flexibility. In Taekwon-Do, incorporating static stretching into your routine helps elongate muscles, which contributes to better kick execution and decreased muscle soreness. After intense training, static stretching facilitates recovery by alleviating tension and promoting muscle relaxation.

A static stretch using the wall to support a high side kick position. This stretch targets the hamstrings, glutes and adductors, helping to improve flexibility and kicking height. Using a wall provides stability, allowing the practitioner to focus on alignment, balance and deepening the stretch. Static stretching is essential for increasing the range of motion and preventing injury in kicking techniques.

### Proprioceptive Neuromuscular Facilitation (PNF)

PNF stretching techniques, such as contract-relax and hold-relax, are renowned for their effectiveness in rapidly increasing flexibility. PNF involves a sequence of muscle contractions and relaxations, targeting both the muscles and neural pathways. This method provides deeper stretches compared to traditional static stretching and enhances kick efficiency. By including PNF stretching in your routine, you can achieve significant gains in flexibility and improve overall kicking performance.

### Active Isolated Stretching

Active isolated stretching focuses on specific muscle groups through controlled, isolated movements. This technique promotes blood flow to the targeted muscles, aiding in tissue repair and recovery while maintaining muscle strength and stability. Incorporating active isolated stretching helps sustain optimal flexibility and mobility, contributing to more effective and controlled kicks during Taekwon-Do training.

### Ballistic Stretching

Ballistic stretching involves rapid, bouncing movements to push muscles beyond their normal range of motion. Research indicates that this type of stretching can lead to muscle damage, strains and decreased flexibility. For Taekwon-Do practitioners, it is advisable to avoid ballistic stretching due to its higher risk of injury. Instead, focus on safer, more controlled stretching techniques such as dynamic, static, PNF and active isolated stretching.

### Crafting an Effective Stretching Routine

To maximise the benefits of stretching, practitioners should integrate various techniques into their training regimen. A balanced approach includes:

- **Pre-training warm-up** Begin with dynamic stretching to prepare muscles and joints for the demands of Taekwon-Do practice. This enhances performance and reduces the risk of injury.
- **Post-training cool-down** Follow up with static stretching to relax muscles, improve flexibility and facilitate recovery after intense training sessions.
- **Regular flexibility work** Incorporate PNF and active isolated stretching into your routine to achieve deeper flexibility and maintain mobility.
- **Avoidance of ballistic stretching** Refrain from using ballistic stretching due to its potential for injury. Opt for safer, scientifically supported methods instead.

## OPTIMISING MUSCLE ACTIVATION FOR EFFECTIVE KICKING

Muscle activation is a critical component of effective kicking in Taekwon-Do and other martial arts. It involves engaging specific muscle groups to ensure that each kick is powerful, precise and performed with optimal efficiency while minimising the risk of injury.

At its core, muscle activation refers to the engagement of particular muscles necessary for executing a movement. For kicking, this means not only initiating the kick with primary muscles but also using supporting muscles to stabilise and control the movement. Proper activation ensures that the kick is performed with the required strength and control.

Several key muscle groups are integral to kicking. The hip flexors, including the iliopsoas and rectus femoris, are responsible for lifting the leg. Engaging these muscles helps in raising the leg efficiently and with speed. The quadriceps play a crucial role in extending the knee during the kick. Activation of the quadriceps ensures that the kick has the necessary force and that the leg remains straight throughout the motion.

The hamstrings contribute by controlling the leg's movement and stabilising the hip joint during the kick. Proper activation of the hamstrings aids in decelerating the leg after the kick and preparing for subsequent movements. The glutes, particularly the gluteus maximus, generate significant power for the kick and help stabilise the pelvis and hip throughout the motion.

Core muscles, including the abdominals and obliques, are essential for maintaining balance and stability during a kick. A strong core facilitates the transfer of power from the lower body through the torso into the kick. Additionally, the calf muscles assist in foot propulsion, providing extra power and stability during the kicking motion. Proper activation of the calves helps achieve the desired height and distance for the kick.

To enhance muscle activation, several techniques can be employed. Warming up with dynamic exercises such as leg swings, high knees and hip circles prepares the relevant muscle groups for the demands of kicking. Specific kicking drills that focus on muscle engagement train the body to activate the necessary muscles effectively. Strength training exercises like squats, lunges, and leg presses build the strength and activation of muscles used in kicking, thereby improving overall power.

Attention to technique is also crucial. By focusing on proper kicking form, practitioners ensure that the correct muscles are engaged. For instance, engaging the core and glutes during a kick improves power and control. Developing a strong mind-muscle connection by consciously focusing on the muscles being used can further enhance muscle activation.

Recovery plays an essential role in maintaining effective muscle activation. Post-training practices such as stretching, foam rolling and sufficient rest help relieve muscle tension and ensure that muscles remain responsive for future training sessions. This not only aids in recovery but also contributes to sustained performance and injury prevention.

Understanding the roles of mobility and flexibility, and incorporating effective stretching techniques, are crucial for Taekwon-Do practitioners aiming to enhance performance and prevent injuries. By implementing dynamic and static stretching, as well as advanced methods like PNF and active isolated stretching, you can achieve greater flexibility, improved kick execution, and a reduced risk of injury. With consistent practice and attention to proper technique, you will build a solid foundation for powerful and precise kicks, contributing to overall success in Taekwon-Do.

A side kick executed with precision – hips aligned, foot sword extended and posture controlled. This technique combines power, balance and timing to deliver a strong, linear strike capable of stopping an opponent in their tracks. Clean form, sharp intent.

# 6 INJURY PREVENTION AND RECOVERY IN TAEKWON-DO KICKING

In Taekwon-Do, kicking forms a cornerstone of both offensive and defensive strategies. The practice of drilling kicks, while essential for honing technique and power, places significant demands on the body. To ensure a long and successful martial arts career, it is crucial to implement effective injury prevention and recovery strategies. This chapter explores both practical and scientific methods for safeguarding against injuries and promoting optimal recovery after intensive kicking drills.

## COMMON KICKING INJURIES

Kicking injuries commonly affect several areas of the body. Muscle strains are prevalent, often occurring in the hamstrings, quadriceps, adductors and hip flexors due to overexertion or improper technique. Joint injuries, particularly to the knees, hips and ankles, can arise from repetitive high-impact kicks. Tendonitis, an inflammation of tendons around these joints, is another frequent issue, caused by repetitive stress. Additionally, bruising and contusions may result from direct impacts with hard surfaces or incorrect kicking techniques.

## INJURY PREVENTION STRATEGIES

The foundation of injury prevention lies in mindfully performing the correct kicking technique. Practitioners must ensure that their form is precise, aligning their body correctly to avoid undue stress on muscles and joints. Regular feedback from a qualified instructor is invaluable for refining technique and making necessary adjustments.

A thorough warm-up is essential before engaging in intensive kicking drills. Dynamic warm-up exercises, such as leg swings, high knees and hip circles,

A well-executed pressing kick targeting the opponent's knee – controlled, deliberate and effective. This low-line technique uses downward pressure to unbalance or disable, relying on accuracy, stability, and timing rather than speed. A smart, strategic application of force.

help increase blood flow to the muscles and prepare the body for the physical demands of kicking. Following training, a cool-down routine should be performed to gradually lower the body's intensity. This includes light aerobic activity and gentle stretching to help muscles return to their resting state.

To prevent injuries, it is important to increase the intensity and volume of kicking drills gradually. Avoid sudden spikes in training load, which can lead to overuse injuries. Incorporating a variety of kicking drills helps prevent the overuse of specific muscle groups and contributes to a more balanced training regimen.

Strengthening the core, hips and legs is crucial for supporting the demands of kicking. Regular strength-training exercises, such as squats, lunges and leg presses, build the necessary muscle strength. Flexibility training, including both static and dynamic stretches, enhances muscle elasticity and reduces tension, further helping to prevent injuries.

## RECOVERY TECHNIQUES

Post-training, engaging in static stretching is important for alleviating muscle tightness and improving flexibility. Focus on stretching key muscle groups, such as the hamstrings, quadriceps, hip flexors and calves. Additionally, using a foam roller for self-myofascial release can help address areas of muscle soreness and tightness.

Maintaining proper hydration is critical for muscle recovery and to prevent cramps. Drinking water throughout and after training supports overall recovery. A balanced diet rich in proteins, carbohydrates, and healthy fats aids in muscle repair and recovery. Foods high in antioxidants, like berries and leafy greens, can help reduce inflammation.

Incorporating rest days into your training schedule is essential for allowing muscles to recover. Avoid over-training by alternating between intense and moderate sessions. Quality sleep is equally important; aim for seven to nine hours each night to support muscle repair and overall recovery.

For acute injuries, applying the RICE method – Rest, Ice, Compression and Elevation – can effectively reduce swelling and pain. If injuries persist or cause significant discomfort, seeking advice from healthcare professionals or physiotherapists is recommended. They can provide targeted treatment and rehabilitation strategies. In the past, martial artists have been expected to 'tough it out' and train through injuries and sickness, but this is absolutely not the correct way to approach your training. If you need help, go to a qualified professional to support your recovery.

### Scientific Methods of Recovery

Cryotherapy, such as ice baths (which are pretty trendy at the moment) or cold packs, can help reduce muscle soreness and inflammation by constricting blood vessels and decreasing metabolic activity in the affected tissues. This method is effective in managing acute muscle soreness and aiding in faster recovery.

Using compression garments or devices during and after training can enhance blood circulation and reduce swelling, facilitating a quicker recovery process. Compression therapy is beneficial for alleviating muscle soreness and preventing further injury.

Techniques like Transcutaneous Electrical Nerve Stimulation (TENS) involve applying electrical currents to relieve pain and promote muscle recovery. This method can be effective in managing pain and enhancing muscle repair.

Water-based recovery methods, including hot and cold water immersion, can improve circulation and reduce muscle soreness. I personally use this method to recover as I am not an ice bath person! Hydrotherapy offers a soothing way to aid in the recovery process, particularly after intense training sessions, and I have found it brings out any bruising I have much quicker!

Injury prevention and recovery are essential components of effective Taekwon-Do training. Don't neglect your body – it is the only one you'll get! Be mindful to implement proper training routines, including comprehensive warm-ups and cool-downs, and adopt scientifically supported recovery methods. Minimising the risk of injuries and promoting faster recovery not only enhance kicking performance but also contribute to a healthier, more sustainable martial arts practice. As you continue to refine your kicking techniques, remember that maintaining your body's health and well-being is crucial for long-term success and achievement in Taekwon-Do.

# 7 WARMING UP

Before embarking on the explosive techniques of Taekwon-Do kicking, it's imperative to thoroughly prepare your body with an effective warm-up routine. Warming up isn't just a formality; it's a critical aspect of any martial arts training session. Scientific evidence overwhelmingly supports the benefits of a well-executed warm-up. Firstly, it increases blood flow to the muscles, delivering oxygen and essential nutrients while removing waste products. This process primes the muscles for activity, enhancing their flexibility and elasticity, which in turn reduces the risk of strains and injuries during vigorous movements like kicking. A proper warm-up elevates core body temperature, promoting faster nerve impulses and muscle contractions, leading to improved coordination and reaction times.

It is really important to include the right type of stretching and joint mobilisation in your warm-up. Gone are the days of a traditional martial arts class heavy cardio warm-up followed by static stretching, which is proven to do more harm than good, as covered in the previous chapters. Here we will include dynamic stretching in our warm-up to prepare you for your kicking practice and drills.

A good warm-up also prepares practitioners mentally by focusing attention, enhancing concentration and reducing anxiety, thereby optimising performance. This chapter provides a comprehensive warm-up routine tailored specifically to amplify your kicking abilities and elevate your overall Taekwon-Do training experience. Follow the steps below in the order given.

Warming up with resistance bands, activating key muscles for kicking. This targeted prep builds strength, improves mobility and enhances control, ensuring each kick is delivered with power, precision and reduced risk of injury. Preparation is everything.

Ankle rotations are an essential part of a warm-up routine to improve joint mobility and prevent injury. They increase blood flow to the muscles, enhance balance and reduce the risk of sprains by loosening the ligaments and tendons. Proper ankle mobility is crucial for maintaining stability and control during kicking techniques and dynamic movements in Taekwon-Do.

Hip rotations, another vital warm-up exercise to increase mobility and prepare the body for dynamic movements. They help loosen the hip joints, improve flexibility and enhance balance, which is essential for executing powerful kicks. This movement also reduces the risk of injury by promoting joint stability and increasing blood flow to the surrounding muscles.

## JOINT ROTATIONS

Follow this drill for 5 minutes:

1. Begin by rotating your ankles in a circular motion, first clockwise and then anticlockwise, to loosen up the ankle joint.
2. Move on to knee rotations, bending one knee at a time and rotating it in a circular motion to improve flexibility.
3. Perform hip rotations by standing with your feet shoulder-width apart and rotating your hips in a circular motion.
4. Finish with shoulder rotations, moving your shoulders in a circular motion to warm up the upper body.

Skipping as a warm-up exercise, an effective way to elevate heart rate, improve coordination and activate muscles. Skipping increases cardiovascular endurance, enhances footwork and promotes agility, which are essential for martial arts movements. It also helps to loosen joints and reduce the risk of injury by preparing the body for more dynamic activities in training or competition.

## CARDIOVASCULAR WARM-UP

Follow this drill for 5 minutes:

1. Begin with 1 minute of jumping jacks to elevate your heart rate and warm up your entire body.
2. Jog in place for 2 minutes, focusing on staying light on your feet and maintaining a steady rhythm.
3. You can further warm up by skipping for 2–3 minutes.
4. Finish with one minute of high knees to engage your core and hip flexors.

## DYNAMIC STRETCHING

Follow this drill for 7 minutes:

1. Start with leg swings, standing beside a wall for support and swinging one leg forward and backward to stretch the hamstrings and hip flexors.
2. Next, perform front leg raises by lifting one leg straight in front of you to stretch the quadriceps and hip flexors.
3. Follow up with side leg raises, lifting one leg straight out to the side to target the abductors and outer thigh muscles.
4. Finish with back leg raises. Using the wall for support, stand square on facing the wall and swing your leg behind you.

## KICKING-SPECIFIC MOVEMENTS

Follow this drill for 8 minutes:

1. Practise the roundhouse kick motion, focusing on hip rotation and foot positioning without making contact.
2. Perform the front snap kick motion, emphasising the extension and retraction of the leg with proper form.
3. Execute the side kick motion, paying attention to chambering and extension for power and balance.

These three kicks between them cover the right positions for a majority of the other kicks during the warm-up.

## THE IMPORTANCE OF COOLING DOWN

Just as a proper warm-up prepares the body for training, an effective cool-down is essential for recovery and injury prevention. Cooling down helps gradually lower the heart rate, flush out metabolic waste, and maintain flexibility by preventing muscle stiffness.

A structured cool-down should include low-intensity movement followed by static stretching, focusing on the muscles used during training. This allows the body to transition from high-intensity exertion to a restful state, reducing the risk of soreness and promoting long-term flexibility and mobility.

The following cool-down routine provides a simple but effective way to aid recovery after intense kicking practice.

## COOL-DOWN (5 MINUTES)

1. After completing the warm-up routine and any specific training, take a moment to catch your breath and reflect on your practice.
2. If you were to finish at this point, you would continue with the cool-down phase to ensure proper recovery and flexibility.
3. Begin the cool-down with light static stretching, focusing on the muscles used during kicking, such as the hamstrings, quadriceps and hip flexors.
4. Hold each stretch for 15–30 seconds, breathing deeply and relaxing into the stretch to release tension and promote flexibility.

# PART 2

# INTRODUCTION TO THE FUNDAMENTAL KICKS IN ITF TAEKWON-DO

# 8 THE FRONT KICK

The front kick, *ap chagi* in Korean, is one of the foundational kicks in Taekwon-Do, and is a simple but effective linear kick. In this chapter, we will delve into the intricacies of this kick, from its fundamental elements to advanced applications, equipping you with the knowledge to execute it correctly with precision and power.

## FUNDAMENTAL ELEMENTS

All kicks follow the same execution: chamber, extension, rechamber.

The front kick is designed to attack an opponent in front of you. It is executed by lifting the knee high into the chamber position, thrusting the foot forward and striking the target with the ball of the foot, instep, toes or knee. Once executed, the kick is retracted back to your fighting stance or in ITF Taekwon-Do pattern, ready for the next move in the choreography. It involves engaging the hip flexors and extending the leg swiftly, generating force from the lower body.

The front kick can be used both offensively and defensively in various situations. It commonly targets the groin, torso, abdomen or face of an opponent. The trajectory of the kick should be direct and linear (reaching the target in a straight line), while taking care to minimise telegraphing the kick and maximising speed.

The high front kick showcases technical discipline and dynamic range. Striking with the ball of the foot, it delivers direct force to a vulnerable target, blending sharp mechanics with focused intent.

**The front kick** The chamber is the initial phase of the front kick, where the knee lifts high towards the chest to prepare for the strike. This position engages the hip flexors and stores potential energy, which is crucial for generating power in the kick. A well-executed chamber improves balance, minimises telegraphing and ensures the kick travels in a direct, linear trajectory toward the target.

The execution phase of the front kick involves thrusting the foot forward from the chamber position to strike the target. The kick should be direct and swift, with the striking surface depending on the target – ball of the foot, instep, toes or knee. Proper execution requires hip engagement and core stability to maximise force while maintaining balance and control.

The rechamber phase is the retraction of the leg after delivering the front kick. This step is essential for maintaining balance and preparing for the next move. Rechambering quickly prevents the leg from being caught by an opponent and allows the practitioner to return to their fighting stance or prepare for the next technique in a pattern, maintaining flow and readiness in movement.

## TYPES OF FRONT KICK

Practitioners have various styles of front kick they can perform, with snapping and thrusting being the most common.

The front snapping kick *(apcha busigi)* can be used low and middle. The striking tool is most often the ball of the foot and the toes, but it can be performed explosively using various striking tools:

- **Ball of the foot** For strikes to the groin or solar plexus at a normal distance, with the toes pulled back to produce the ball of the foot. The ankle should be plantar flexing, with the toes extending upward.
- **Toes** Only used to attack the groin at a normal distance, with all the toes straight and the ankle plantar flexed. Best performed with shoes on.
- **Knee** Used to attack an opponent at close quarters, thrusting up to the opponent's abdomen or groin.
- **Instep** Used to attack an opponent to the groin at close quarters using the top of the foot.

In ITF patterns, the front kick is often performed with specific technical guidelines, especially for an athlete who is looking to compete at an elite level. There is an emphasis on scoring for technical content, balance, control and proper form.

The knee being used as the striking tool.

A middle front snapping kick, aimed at the torso of an opponent. The kick is delivered explosively, with the ball of the foot as the primary striking tool. This technique is versatile, used to target vital areas like the solar plexus or abdomen, causing significant impact while maintaining speed, balance and control during execution.

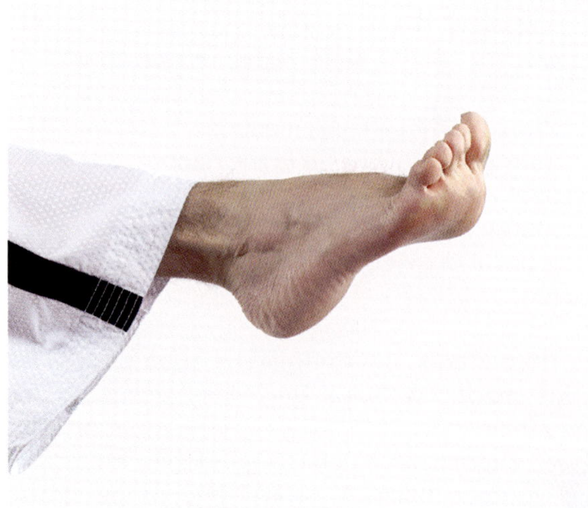

The ball of the foot being used as the striking tool.

The toes being used as the striking tool.

A front push kick, which focuses on power and forward penetration. Using the hips to thrust the kicking leg straight out, this technique aims to push an opponent back or deliver a powerful strike to the midsection or chest. The front push kick is effective for creating distance or disrupting an opponent's balance with a forceful, linear motion.

The ITF pattern front snapping kick is executed with the standing foot pointing forward, keeping the body upright with a weight drop into the kick. The side front snap kick is used to attack someone to the side of you and is normally executed from L-stance, rear foot or vertical stance with the body half facing. In ITF patterns there are no high front kicks, only low or middle; the kick is intended for a close target so the leg never fully extends.

The pushing front kick, also known as a front push kick, emphasises power and penetration. This style involves using the hips to thrust the kicking leg straight out with force, aiming to drive the foot into the target, making it effective for pushing opponents back or delivering powerful strikes to the midsection or chest. In contrast, the snapping front kick focuses on speed and precision, utilising a quick, snapping motion followed by a rapid retraction using the ball of the foot or shin in self-defence application. It targets vulnerable areas such as the groin, solar plexus or face, aiming to surprise opponents with swift and precise strikes.

## COMPARING FRONT SNAP AND PUSH KICKS

| | **Front snap kick** | **Front push kick** |
|---|---|---|
| **Execution** | Knee chambers up, then leg extends forward with ball of foot striking target | Knee chambers high and the leg extends forward with foot flat or slightly angled, pushing target away |
| **Target** | Solar plexus, ribs, face and groin | Midsection, chest, knees and thighs |
| **Purpose** | Quick, direct strike for damage or scoring points | Maintaining distance, disrupting balance, controlling opponent's movement |
| **Application** | Inflicting damage, creating openings in sparring | Creating space, controlling distance |
| **Force** | Forceful strike | Pushing force |
| **Follow-up potential** | Sets up for follow-up techniques | Creates space for subsequent movements |

# MUSCLES USED IN FRONT KICKS

In Taekwon-Do, doing a front kick means using lots of different muscles in your body. From the big ones like your thighs to the smaller ones in your feet, they all play a part in making your kick strong and precise. So, before you start practising or using front kicks in your training, it's really important to warm up properly.

## MUSCLE GROUPS ENGAGED IN A TAEKWON-DO FRONT KICK

| Muscle | Use in kick |
|---|---|
| **Quadriceps** | These muscles at the front of your thighs are crucial for extending your leg and providing power for the kick |
| **Hip flexors** | These muscles, located at the front of the hips, are engaged in lifting the knee and initiating the kick motion |
| **Core muscles** | Muscles of the core, including the abdominals and obliques, stabilise your body during the kick and help maintain balance and control |
| **Hamstrings** | These muscles at the back of the thighs play a role in stabilising the leg during the kick and controlling its movement |
| **Glutes** | The gluteal muscles, particularly the gluteus maximus, are involved in extending the hip and providing power to the kick |
| **Calves** | The calf muscles are engaged in stabilising the ankle and foot, providing support during the kick's extension |
| **Adductors** | These muscles in the groin help maintain balance and control by preventing excessive outward movement of the leg as the kicking leg extends forward |
| **Flexor muscles of the foot** | These muscles help point the toes and generate speed at the end of the kick |

## Dynamic Stretching and Mobility Routine

Before practising the front kick, it is crucial that you warm up your muscles with dynamic stretches such as front leg swings, leg crescents, hip circles, hamstring scoops and knee raises. These movements prepare the body for the dynamic motions involved in kicking while reducing the risk of injury.

**Leg swings** Front leg swings improve dynamic flexibility by actively engaging the hip flexors and hamstrings. Stand upright with feet shoulder-width apart. Swing one leg forward and backward, focusing on a controlled motion. Gradually increase the height of each swing while maintaining balance. For additional support, hold on to a stable surface. Perform ten to fifteen swings per leg to warm up the lower body effectively.

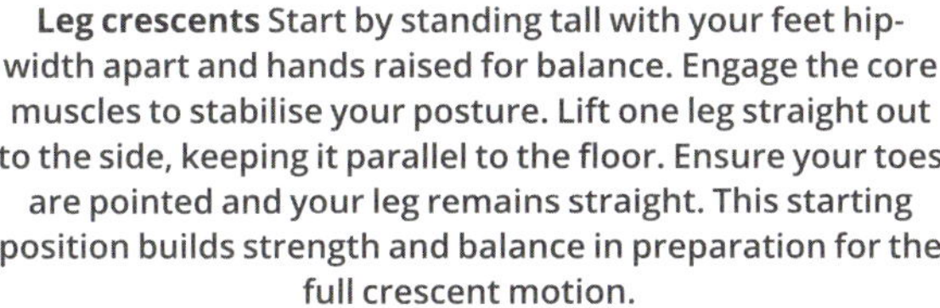

**Leg crescents** Start by standing tall with your feet hip-width apart and hands raised for balance. Engage the core muscles to stabilise your posture. Lift one leg straight out to the side, keeping it parallel to the floor. Ensure your toes are pointed and your leg remains straight. This starting position builds strength and balance in preparation for the full crescent motion.

Swing your extended leg smoothly across your body in a controlled arc, creating a crescent shape. Aim to bring your foot towards your opposite hand, maintaining a steady and fluid movement. Focus on engaging your core to keep your upper body steady while allowing your hips to rotate naturally to support the movement.

Once your leg reaches the opposite side of your body, return it to the starting position with control. Keep your core engaged throughout to maintain balance. Ensure your movements are precise, avoiding any jerking motion. Perform eight to ten leg crescents on each side to improve flexibility, balance and coordination in kicking techniques.

**Hip circles/rotations** Stand with feet shoulder-width apart and hands on your hips for balance. Slowly rotate your hips in a circular motion, starting clockwise, making large, controlled circles. Keep your core engaged and knees slightly bent to avoid strain. Perform ten rotations in each direction. This exercise enhances hip mobility, loosens tight muscles and improves balance and coordination, which are essential for martial arts.

**Knee raises** Stand upright with feet hip-width apart and maintain a strong posture. Lift one knee towards the chest, ensuring your thigh is parallel to the ground. Engage your core to stabilise your body as you hold the position briefly. Lower the leg back down with control. Repeat ten to twelve times on each leg to improve balance and hip mobility.

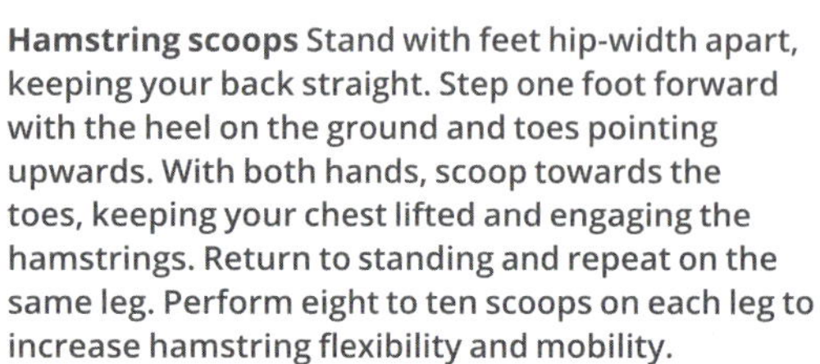

**Hamstring scoops** Stand with feet hip-width apart, keeping your back straight. Step one foot forward with the heel on the ground and toes pointing upwards. With both hands, scoop towards the toes, keeping your chest lifted and engaging the hamstrings. Return to standing and repeat on the same leg. Perform eight to ten scoops on each leg to increase hamstring flexibility and mobility.

## CORRECT TECHNIQUE AND BIOMECHANICAL PRINCIPLES

A front kick involves coordinated joint movements and muscle engagement to generate power and maintain balance. Below is a concise breakdown of its key biomechanical components:

1. **Stance and initiation** Begin in a neutral stance with feet shoulder-width apart. Shift weight to the supporting leg for balance.
2. **Chambering** Lift the kicking leg by bending the knee and bringing the foot towards the chest. This activates the hip flexors and prepares for the kick.
3. **Extension** Drive the foot forward by rapidly extending the knee. The quadriceps power this motion.
4. **Foot positioning** The foot is either dorsiflexed (toes up) or neutral. For striking with the ball of the foot, point the toes downward.
5. **Hip action** The hip undergoes flexion, abduction and internal rotation, increasing the kick's reach and power.
6. **Trunk rotation** In some styles (such as Taekwon-Do), slight trunk rotation adds torque and increases the kick's impact, especially for pushing kicks.
7. **Balance and stability** The supporting leg and core muscles stabilise the body throughout the movement to prevent excessive sway.
8. **Breathing** Exhale forcefully at the point of impact to enhance power, coordination, and focus.
9. **Follow-through** After striking, retract the kicking leg to maintain control. The degree of follow-through depends on the style.

Understanding the biomechanics of a front kick allows practitioners to refine their technique, improve efficiency and maximise the effectiveness of their kicks. By focusing on proper body mechanics and incorporating specific training drills, martial artists can improve their front kicks and excel in combat situations.

The foot of the standing leg should remain grounded. In Taekwon-Do patterns, the foot on the standing leg should remain pointing forward and the hands need to remain as the Taekwon-Do Encyclopaedia directs, but for sparring or bag work technique you can pivot the standing foot to open up the hips allowing for more thrust and power.

## EXAMPLES OF INCORRECT TECHNIQUE

Incorrect technique in Taekwon-Do's front kick can significantly compromise its effectiveness and efficiency. Here are some common mistakes practitioners might make:

- **Telegraphing the kick** This refers to unintentionally signalling the upcoming kick to the opponent, typically by dropping the guard or making any other movement that gives away the intention to kick. Telegraphing allows the opponent to anticipate and potentially counter the kick effectively.
- **Insufficient chambering** In the initial phase of the kick, the knee is raised towards the chest before extending the leg to execute the kick. If the chambering is not high enough, it reduces the power and reach of the kick, making it easier for the opponent to defend against or counter.
- **Incorrect trajectory** The trajectory of the kick is crucial for both power and accuracy. If the leg is not extended along the correct path, it can result in diminished power and compromised targeting. Kicking too high or too low from the intended target area can also reduce effectiveness.
- **Incorrect foot shape** Holding the foot correctly upon impact is essential for maximising the effectiveness of the kick. Using the incorrect foot shape, for example not properly pointing the toes or not flexing the foot upon impact, can lead to less effective strikes and increase the risk of injury to both the kicker and the opponent.

- **Making the kick too soft or weak** This error happens when the practitioner doesn't put enough power into their front kick. While it's important to be careful during practice or when sparring with beginners, kicking too gently can mean the kick won't have the impact it needs in a real fight. A weak kick might not stop or hurt your opponent enough, letting them keep fighting or defend themselves easily. It's important to kick with enough strength to do what you need while still being accurate and controlled.
- **Overextending the leg** This occurs when the leg is fully extended too early in the kicking motion, leaving it vulnerable to being blocked or countered by the opponent. Overextending also reduces the power and control of the kick, making it less effective in delivering a significant impact.
- **Incomplete rechamber** After extending the kick, failing to bring the leg back swiftly to the starting position leaves it exposed and vulnerable to counter-attacks. An incomplete rechamber also delays the practitioner's ability to follow up with additional strikes or defensive manoeuvres, compromising balance and safety.
- **Leaning backwards** Leaning backwards during the execution of the front kick shifts the body's weight away from the target, reducing the effectiveness and power of the strike. This posture also compromises balance and stability, increasing the risk of being easily pushed off balance or countered by the opponent.
- **Unbalanced standing foot** Failing to maintain balance upon landing the kick can lead to instability and vulnerability to counter-attacks.

In Taekwon-Do, the correct technique is essential for maximising the power, speed, and precision of each kick while minimising the risk of injury. Proper training and attention to detail are crucial in correcting these common mistakes and refining front kick technique.

A front kick performed with poor equilibrium, incorrect trajectory, and improper hip and foot positioning. The practitioner leans back excessively, causing a loss of balance and reducing the kick's effectiveness. The hips are not fully engaged to drive the kick forward, and the foot shape lacks proper alignment for striking. These errors can compromise power, control and accuracy in execution.

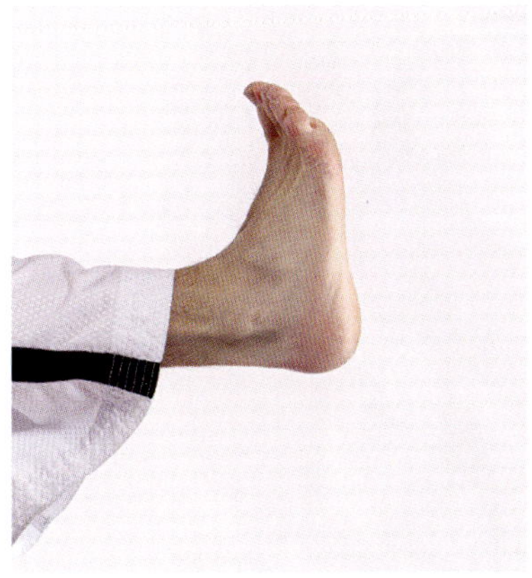

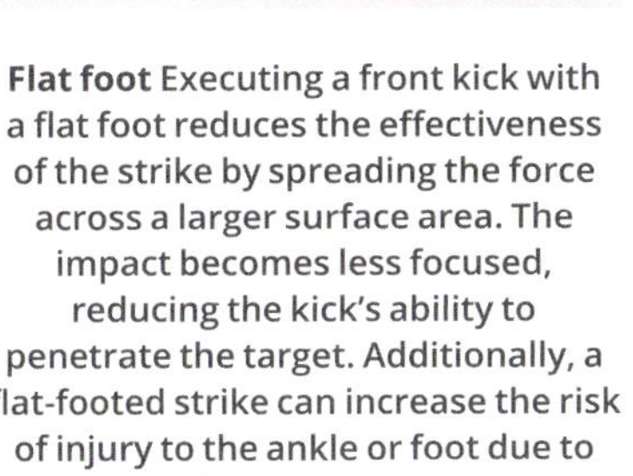

**Flat foot** Executing a front kick with a flat foot reduces the effectiveness of the strike by spreading the force across a larger surface area. The impact becomes less focused, reducing the kick's ability to penetrate the target. Additionally, a flat-footed strike can increase the risk of injury to the ankle or foot due to improper alignment upon contact.

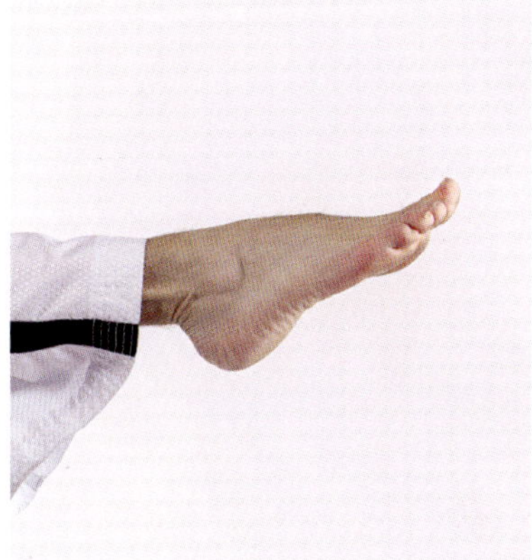

**Pointed toes** Keeping the toes pointed during a front kick reduces the striking surface area and makes the strike less effective. While it may appear aesthetically correct, it compromises power and precision, especially for kicks aimed at the torso or face; the toes should only be used for a kick to the groin. Pointed toes also increase the risk of toe injuries upon impact.

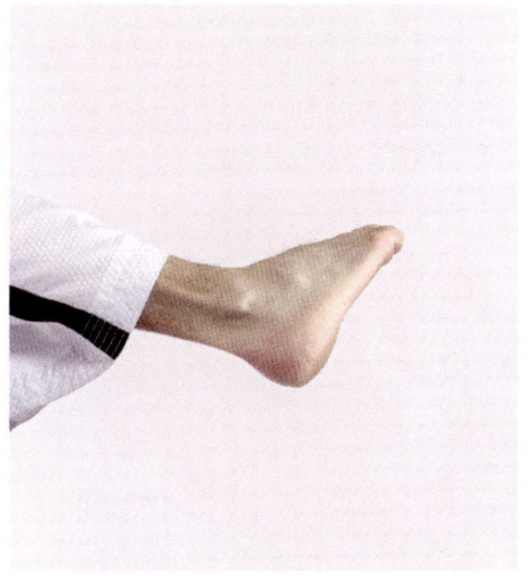

**Skewed foot** A skewed foot position during a front kick can lead to ineffective strikes and increased injury risk. Pressing the sword of the foot forward, rather than the ball, reduces the kick's power and precision. Proper foot shape ensures that the impact is delivered through the correct striking tool, maximising force and reducing the likelihood of damaging the toes or ankle upon contact.

## BASIC STRENGTH, MOBILITY AND CONDITIONING EXERCISES

Think of flexibility as how much you can stretch, like a rubber band. Mobility is how smoothly your joints move, like a well-oiled machine. Flexibility is about stretching muscles, mobility is about moving joints.

Enhance the power and strength of your front kick by incorporating exercises that strengthen the hip flexors, quadriceps and core muscles. Ensure a proper warm-up before engaging in strength and conditioning exercises, and consult with a personal trainer to verify correct form and technique.

Strength-training exercises for improving the front kick in martial arts should focus on enhancing the power, stability and flexibility of the muscles involved. Here are some exercises that can help, along with instructions for each:

### Lower Body Strength Exercises

Incorporate these exercises into your training routine to improve the power, stability and effectiveness of your front kick. Start slow and use manageable weight initially; consistency and progressive overload are key for continual improvement in strength and power for martial arts techniques like the front kick. Always prioritise proper form to prevent injury. Make sure you consult a personal trainer for a specific programme of strength and conditioning training.

## POWER TESTING WITH THE FRONT KICK

In Taekwon-Do, the front kick doesn't just involve precision and speed; it also requires the ability to generate significant power, especially when used in bag work and power-breaking techniques.

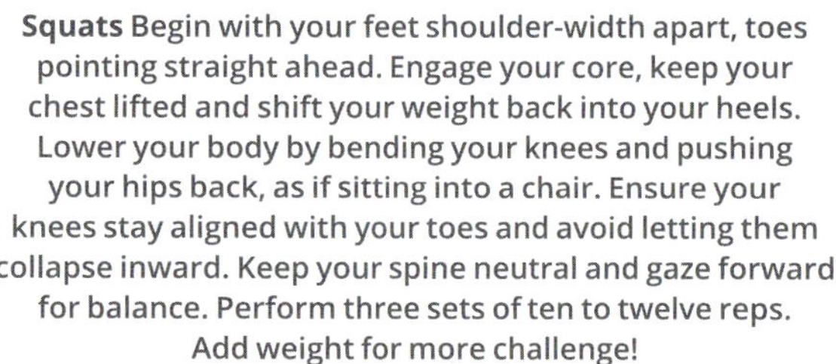

**Squats** Begin with your feet shoulder-width apart, toes pointing straight ahead. Engage your core, keep your chest lifted and shift your weight back into your heels. Lower your body by bending your knees and pushing your hips back, as if sitting into a chair. Ensure your knees stay aligned with your toes and avoid letting them collapse inward. Keep your spine neutral and gaze forward for balance. Perform three sets of ten to twelve reps. Add weight for more challenge!

**Lunges** Begin by standing upright with your feet hip-width apart, shoulders back, and core engaged. Take a controlled step forward with your right foot, ensuring your torso remains upright and your front knee aligns over your ankle. Maintain a neutral spine throughout the movement to avoid strain. For added resistance, hold dumbbells at your sides with a firm grip.

Lower your body by bending both knees into a lunge position, keeping your balance steady and core engaged. Push through your front heel to return to standing. Perform three sets of eight to twelve reps on each leg. If using weights, keep dumbbells at your sides or on your shoulders, ensuring they don't affect your posture or balance during the exercise.

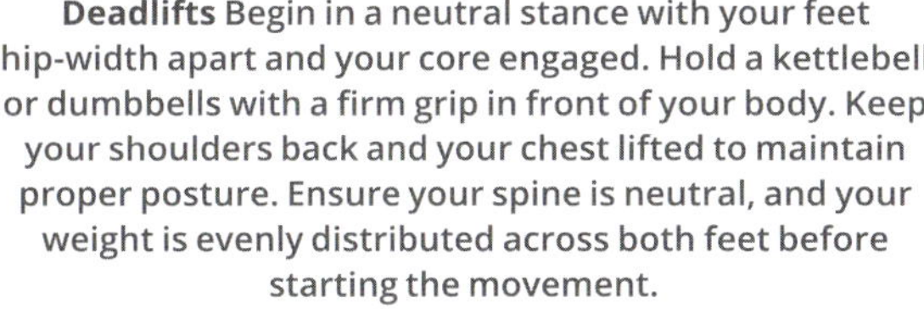

**Deadlifts** Begin in a neutral stance with your feet hip-width apart and your core engaged. Hold a kettlebell or dumbbells with a firm grip in front of your body. Keep your shoulders back and your chest lifted to maintain proper posture. Ensure your spine is neutral, and your weight is evenly distributed across both feet before starting the movement.

Hinge at your hips and bend your knees to lower the weight toward the floor, keeping it close to your body. Keep your back straight and your chest lifted throughout the movement. Push through your heels to return to the standing position. Perform three sets of six to eight reps. Hold the dumbbells or kettlebell securely to maintain balance and control.

**Glute bridge** Lie flat on your back with your knees bent and feet flat on the floor, hip-width apart. Keep your arms relaxed at your sides. Drive through your heels to lift your hips towards the ceiling, squeezing your glutes at the top of the movement. Lower your hips back to the ground with control. Perform three sets of ten to twelve reps to strengthen the glutes and improve hip stability.

**Plank** Begin in a plank position with your forearms on the floor and elbows directly beneath your shoulders. Engage your core muscles and maintain a straight line from your head to your heels. Keep your hips level, avoiding any sagging or lifting. Hold the plank for 30–60 seconds to strengthen your core and stabilise your posture. Perform three sets.

**Russian twists** Sit on the ground with your knees bent and feet flat on the floor. Lean back slightly, keeping your back straight, and hold a weight or medicine ball with both hands. Rotate your torso to the right, bringing the weight beside your hip, then return to the centre. Repeat the movement to the left side. Complete three sets of twelve to fifteen reps per side.

**Front kick pulses** Lean your back against a wall for balance, or perform without wall support for an advanced version, as demonstrated. Extend your front kick to its highest point and pulse the leg up and down ten times with small, controlled movements. Rechamber your leg and repeat. Perform three sets of twelve to fifteen reps on each leg to improve kicking height and control.

**Front kick holds** Stand with your back against a wall to maintain balance, or perform without wall support to challenge your stability and core strength, as demonstrated. Extend your front kick as high as possible, keeping your core engaged and posture upright. Hold the leg for ten seconds. Rechamber and repeat. Perform three sets of twelve to fifteen reps on each leg to build strength and endurance.

Bag work and power breaking demonstrate the practitioner's ability to channel maximum force into a single strike, starting with bag work and working towards breaking wooden boards. Here's how to perform bag work and power break with the front kick effectively:

1. **Focus on technique** Before adding power, ensure your front kick technique is flawless. Practise the fundamental elements repeatedly until they become second nature. Pay close attention to your stance, hip rotation and extension of the leg.
2. **Visualise the target** See the target you intend to strike or break in your mind before unleashing your kick. Whether it's a wooden board, a kickshield or another object, visualise yourself striking through it with precision and power.

This mental focus can enhance your confidence and determination.

3. **Generate momentum** Power in a front kick comes from the swift extension of the leg and the push of the hip. Start by generating momentum from your lower body, engaging your core muscles to facilitate a rapid extension of the leg.
4. **Drive from the hip** The power in your front kick originates from the hip flexors. As you execute the kick, drive your hip forward forcefully, transferring the energy from your body into the target. This hip thrust adds significant power to your kick.
5. **Snap the leg** Focus on snapping your leg forward at the moment of impact. This snapping action not only adds speed to your kick but also concentrates the force onto a smaller area of the target, increasing the likelihood of a successful break.
6. **Control your breathing** Coordinate your breathing with the execution of the kick. Inhale as you chamber your leg and exhale forcefully as you extend it towards the target. This controlled exhalation can enhance the power and focus of your kick.
7. **Commit and follow through** Fully commit to the kick. Once you initiate the kick, follow through completely, ensuring that your foot penetrates the target with maximum force. Maintain your focus until the kick is complete.
8. **Progress gradually** Start practising on kick shields and move up to power breaking set-ups, such as breaking a single reusable breaker board, before progressing to more boards or challenging techniques. Gradually increase the thickness or number of boards as your power and technique improve.

## STATIC STRETCHING FOR FLEXIBILITY

After your training session, engage in static stretches targeting the hip flexors, hamstrings and calf muscles to enhance flexibility and reduce muscle tension. Hold each stretch for 20–30 seconds, breathing deeply and gradually increasing the stretch. As time progresses, hold the stretch for longer periods.

**Front kick power breaking** Demonstrating precision and force, the front kick uses the ball of the foot to break through the board in a synthesis of power, balance and technique.

Using a Taekwon-Do belt, this passive stretch focuses on improving hamstring flexibility. The stretch is held with minimal muscular effort, allowing for a deeper range of motion while maintaining proper alignment and control. Ideal for post-training recovery or improving kicking height.

## Types of Static Stretching

**Active static stretching** involves using your own muscle strength to hold a stretched position by engaging the muscles opposite to those being stretched. This method helps improve flexibility and range of motion by training the muscles to relax and elongate over time. An example of active static stretching in Taekwon-Do is holding a front kick at maximum height and maintaining that position for a set period, which builds both strength and control in the kicking muscles.

**Passive static stretching** relies on external assistance, such as gravity, a partner or a prop, to maintain the stretch position without active muscle engagement. This type of stretching improves flexibility and range of motion by elongating muscles and connective tissues through the support of an outside force. Common examples include using a strap to pull your leg closer in a seated forward bend or placing your leg against a wall to support a hip flexor stretch.

Both types of stretching can be beneficial for improving flexibility and range of motion when performed correctly and consistently.

## Static Stretching Routine for Front Kick

**Seated hamstring stretch** This stretch focuses on improving hamstring flexibility by lengthening the muscles along the back of your thighs. Begin seated with your legs extended straight out in front of you. Hinge forward at your hips, reaching towards your toes without rounding your back. Hold the stretch for 20–30 seconds, ensuring you feel a gentle pull in the hamstrings. Repeat this stretch two to three times to maximise flexibility.

**Elevated hamstring stretch** Elevate one leg on a stable object. Flex your foot towards your shin to intensify the stretch. Hold this position for 20–30 seconds, ensuring your leg stays straight. Switch sides and perform two to three sets on each leg for balanced flexibility.

**Low lunge** The low lunge is excellent for stretching the hip flexors and thighs while improving lower-body mobility. Begin in a kneeling position. Step one foot forward with the front knee at a 90-degree angle. Sink your hips forwards and down, feeling a deep stretch in the front of your hip and thigh. Hold for 20–30 seconds, then switch sides. Perform two to three sets on each leg for flexibility.

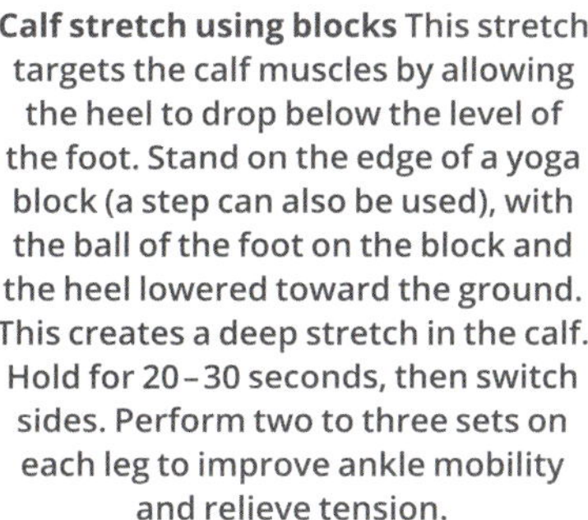

**Calf stretch using blocks** This stretch targets the calf muscles by allowing the heel to drop below the level of the foot. Stand on the edge of a yoga block (a step can also be used), with the ball of the foot on the block and the heel lowered toward the ground. This creates a deep stretch in the calf. Hold for 20–30 seconds, then switch sides. Perform two to three sets on each leg to improve ankle mobility and relieve tension.

**Deep squat holds** Improve hip mobility and ankle flexibility with deep squat holds. Stand with your feet shoulder-width apart and lower yourself into a deep squat position. Keep your chest up and your heels flat on the ground. Hold this position for 20–30 seconds, maintaining balance and control. Return to a standing position and repeat. Perform two to three sets to increase lower-body flexibility and strength.

**Pigeon pose** The pigeon pose is ideal for stretching the hips and glutes, releasing tension in these areas. Start in a plank position, bringing one knee forward towards the same-side wrist. Adjust the front shin to be as parallel to the mat as possible. Extend the opposite leg behind you. Hold for 30–60 seconds, ensuring your hips are aligned. Switch sides and repeat for two to three sets.

**Knee-to-chest stretch** Release tension in your lower back and glutes with the knee-to-chest stretch. Lie flat on your back with your legs extended. Bring one knee towards your chest, hugging it gently with both hands. Keep your other leg extended and relaxed on the ground. Hold for 20–30 seconds, then switch sides. Perform two to three sets on each leg to promote flexibility and relieve muscle tightness.

**Adductor foam rolling** Using a foam roller to release tension in the adductors, the inner thigh is positioned over the roller with the leg bent at a 90-degree angle. Roll slowly from the knee to the groin, pausing on tight spots to relieve muscle tension. This technique enhances mobility and supports recovery. Perform 30–60 seconds per side, focusing on keeping the movement controlled and steady.

### Foam Rolling

Use a foam roller to massage and release tension in the muscles of the thighs, hips, and glutes. Roll back and forth over each muscle group, pausing on any tight or tender areas.

Perform foam rolling for 2–3 minutes on each muscle group.

## KEY ELEMENTS COVERED IN THIS CHAPTER

- Fundamental elements: the chamber, extension and rechamber (CER) sequence that is essential for executing a powerful front kick.
- Various styles of front kick, including the snapping front kick and the pushing front kick, each serving specific purposes and targeting different areas
- Technical guidelines for front kick execution in ITF patterns, focusing on balance, control and proper form for competition
- Identification of common mistakes and guidance on correcting the technique to maximise effectiveness
- Strength, mobility and conditioning exercises targeting muscle groups essential for front kick execution
- Techniques for power testing
- Static stretching routines to enhance performance and reduce muscle tension post-training

## LOOKING AHEAD

In the next chapter, we will explore turning kicks, building upon the foundation laid in mastering the front kick to expand the practitioner's repertoire of striking techniques. Stay tuned for an in-depth exploration of this dynamic aspect of Taekwon-Do kicking.

An inward kick delivered with offensive intent, arcing sharply into the opponent's solar plexus. This technique combines speed, precision and a tight line of motion to exploit gaps in the guard, making it an effective close-range strike with disruptive impact.

# 9 | THE TURNING KICK

The turning kick, *dollyo chagi* in Korean or roundhouse kick in other martial arts disciplines, is renowned for its speed, versatility and effectiveness in sparring. The turning kick attacks an opponent either directly in front of you or to the side front. This kick can attack low, middle and high targets and is normally executed off the rear leg for power, but during sparring can be executed off the lead leg for speed and point scoring.

In this chapter, we will delve into the intricacies of the turning kick, dissecting its mechanics, exploring its applications and unveiling various ways to strengthen your turning kick.

## FUNDAMENTAL ELEMENTS

At the heart of every turning kick lies the fundamental sequence of chamber, extension and rechamber (CER). This sequential execution ensures optimal power and precision, serving as the bedrock upon which the technique is built. Without the correct CER in place, the kick will fall victim to numerous technical errors that will compromise power.

Initiating the turning kick involves a coordinated interplay of body mechanics. The pivot on the supporting foot starts the rotational movement, transferring momentum from the lower body to the kicking leg. As the knee rises to the chamber position, potential energy is harnessed, ready to be unleashed upon extension. The leg extends outward in a whip-like circular motion, propelled by the explosive release of stored energy, before swiftly retracting to its original position.

A turning kick in motion, driven by hip rotation and snapped with precision. Striking with the instep or ball of the foot, this technique blends speed, timing and fluid mechanics to deliver a sharp, circular strike capable of catching opponents off-guard. A staple in both sparring and self-defence.

**The turning kick** The kick starts with the chamber. Lift the knee to hip height while maintaining a balanced stance. Start to pivot the supporting foot to initiate rotation, ensuring that the hips align with the intended target. The chamber position is crucial for building potential energy, which will be unleashed during the extension phase of the kick.

During the extension of the turning kick, the leg unfolds in a fluid, circular motion. The striking tool, typically the instep or ball of the foot, is driven toward the target with precision. This phase utilises the rotational momentum created during the chamber, releasing energy to deliver maximum impact while keeping the body controlled and balanced.

Following the extension, swiftly retract the leg into the rechamber position. This phase ensures that the kicking leg returns to a protective stance, maintaining balance and readiness for the next move. Proper rechambering also minimises the risk of counter-attacks by keeping the leg from lingering in an extended position.

Precision is paramount: practitioners must meticulously hone their technique to ensure the trajectory of the kick remains true.

The turning kick epitomises the synthesis of strength and agility, requiring the engagement of core muscles, hip flexors, glutes and leg extensors to generate maximum force while maintaining the fluidity of motion. There will be more about muscles later in the chapter.

Versatility is the hallmark of the turning kick, rendering it indispensable in both offensive and defensive strategies. As an offensive tool, it enables practitioners to target opponents from multiple angles, exploiting openings and creating opportunities for scoring strikes. Whether aiming for the torso, ribs or head, the turning kick can be deployed with efficient effect for point scoring and inflicting significant power upon impact for bag work and power breaking.

Defensively, the turning kick serves as a swift and effective counter-attack against incoming attacks, especially when utilised with evasive footwork. Effectively controlling space and dictating the pace of engagement, practitioners can use the turning kick to maintain distance, frustrate opponents and gain control of the bout.

The fundamental principles of this kick include:

- Swinging the hip forward to allow the foot to arc towards the target
- Ensuring the ball of the foot is vertically aligned with the target upon impact
- Timing the kick so that the foot reaches its highest point just before contact, resulting in slightly downward-pointing toes upon impact
- Positioning the toes of the stationary foot at a 45-degree outward angle at impact
- Keeping the kicking leg as straight as possible at the moment of impact
- Avoiding direct frontal targets during the kick
- Maintaining visibility of the arms throughout the kicking motion

## TYPES OF TURNING KICK

The turning kick *(dollyo chagi)* can be executed at low, middle and high targets, with the ball of the foot and the instep commonly utilised as striking tools. However, it can also be performed explosively and powerfully, employing a variety of striking tools.

The turning kick has a multitude of variations which a martial artist can utilise, each offering unique advantages and challenges:

The ball of the foot is the main striking tool in a turning kick, targeting the face, solar plexus and scrotum primarily, with secondary targets including the armpit, temple and neck.

A high turning kick targeting the face, using the ball of the foot, demands precision and flexibility. The kicking leg chambers high, with a strong pivot on the supporting foot to allow full rotation. The ball of the foot strikes the opponent's face with speed and accuracy, aiming to create a powerful impact while maintaining balance and control.

A middle turning kick targeting the solar plexus, delivered with the ball of the foot, is a precise and powerful technique. The kicking leg chambers high, the hips rotate for full extension, and the supporting foot pivots to allow a smooth rotation. On impact, the ball of the foot drives into the solar plexus, aiming to disrupt the opponent's breathing.

The instep is typically used to target softer areas, such as the neck, jaw or abdomen. When wearing shoes, its effectiveness increases, though the kicking procedure resembles that of the ball of the foot, with toes not pointed downward and a lesser degree of knee bend at impact. A turning kick with the instep can occasionally be used against an opponent standing directly in front of the practitioner, but in most cases, this technique is more effective when executed at a 90-degree angle.

## Rear Leg Turning Kick

The rear leg turning kick is a pivotal technique in martial arts, leveraging the power and reach of the rear leg for powerful strikes. Executed from a stable stance, the kick harnesses the full force generated from the rotation of the hips and torso, delivering a strong strike with the ball of the foot or instep, often targeting vital areas like the ribs or head. Its versatility lies in its ability to swiftly close or create distance, adapting to the flow of a sparring match. Whether utilising it as an offensive attack to dismantle defences or a defensive measure to counter oncoming attacks, effectively executing this kick demands rigorous training in balance, timing and technique. Drills emphasising fluid motion, dynamic attacks and counter-attacks with correct form and footwork are essential for practitioners to integrate the rear leg turning kick into their arsenal, ensuring its efficacy in various sparring scenarios.

## Lead Leg Turning Kick

The lead leg turning kick involves delivering a turning kick with the front leg, offering speed and versatility in sparring situations. Initiated from a fighting stance, the kick uses a swift rotation of the hips and shoulders while extending the lead leg to strike the target with the desired kicking surface, such as the ball of the foot or instep. Commonly targeting the midsection or head of the opponent, the lead leg turning kick can be adjusted in height and angle to suit varying tactical needs. In application, it serves as both an offensive tool, allowing for quick and unexpected attacks to disrupt opponents, and a defensive manoeuvre, creating distance and opportunities for counter-attacks. Effective training focuses on developing leg strength, agility, balance and speed, with an emphasis on precise technique execution. Drills for footwork, timing, and accuracy are essential to learning the lead leg turning kick and using it in sparring scenarios. In sparring, lead leg turning kicks are preferable over rear leg ones, as the kick is faster and less vulnerable.

## Double Turning Kick

The double turning kick involves executing two consecutive turning kicks in quick succession, utilising rotational momentum for power. Initiated with a rotation, the first kick is executed with one leg, followed immediately by the second kick with the same leg. Double targets include the midsection, chest or head, with adjustments made for height and angle; for example, a practitioner could attack the midsection to draw the guard down and then consecutively kick to the head to score the point in sparring. In application, the double turning kick serves both offensive and defensive purposes: overwhelming opponents with rapid strikes while creating and exploiting openings, maintaining distance, deterring opponents, and countering incoming attacks with swift, precise kicks. Effective training focuses on leg strength, agility, balance and flexibility, with an emphasis on smooth transitions and gradual increases in speed. Drills for realistic sparring scenarios could be incorporated to refine the technique under pressure.

# MUSCLES USED IN A TURNING KICK

The execution of a turning kick involves a coordinated effort from various muscle groups to generate power, stability and control throughout the kicking motion. Understanding the specific muscles engaged during this technique is essential for martial artists aiming to optimise their performance and minimise the risk of injury. From the initial wind-up to the extension and follow-through, several muscles play vital roles in executing a powerful and precise turning kick.

## Dynamic Stretching and Mobility Routine

Before practising the turning kick, it is essential to prepare your body with dynamic stretches to enhance flexibility, mobility and circulation while reducing the risk of injury. Incorporate the following dynamic movements into your warm-up routine.

## MUSCLES ENGAGED IN A TURNING KICK

| Muscle group | Function |
|---|---|
| **Quadriceps** | Responsible for extending the knee joint and generating power during the kicking motion |
| **Hamstrings** | Assist in hip extension and stabilise the knee during the kicking phase |
| **Gluteus maximus** | Provides the power for hip extension, which is crucial for generating momentum during the kick |
| **Hip adductors** | Aid in stabilising the hip joint and controlling the inward movement of the kicking leg |
| **Hip abductors** | Assist in controlling the outward movement of the supporting leg and maintaining balance |
| **Gastrocnemius** | Contributes to plantar flexion of the ankle, helping to point the foot and ensure proper alignment during the kick |
| **Soleus** | Stabilises the ankle joint and assists in maintaining balance throughout the kicking motion |
| **Core muscles** | Provide stability and transfer power from the lower body to the upper body, aiding in balance and control |

## COMPARING TURNING KICK VARIATIONS

| Advantages | Rear leg turning kick | Lead leg turning kick | Double turning kick |
|---|---|---|---|
| **Power** | High power due to increased distance and momentum | Moderate power with shorter distance and speed | Potentially double power from two consecutive kicks |
| **Range** | Longer range due to using the rear leg for execution | Shorter range, but quick execution | Versatile range, combining long and short-range kicks |
| **Speed** | Slower due to longer wind-up and travel distance | Faster due to shorter wind-up and execution | Moderate speed, but can be rapid with practice |
| **Versatility** | Suitable for mid- to long-range targets | Quick and suitable for close to mid-range targets | Offers flexibility to adapt to various scenarios |
| **Balance and stability** | Provides stability with a stable stance and controlled pivot | Requires balance and control on the lead leg | Requires good balance and control to execute both kicks smoothly |
| **Defensive manoeuvrability** | Offers a defensive option by creating distance and angle from the opponent | Can be used for quick counters and evasions | Allows for quick counters and evasions with two consecutive kicks |
| **Vulnerability** | Opponent can attack you when you pivot and become full facing | Your balance can be disrupted by the opponent rushing you | |

The stretches outlined in Part 2, Chapter 1, specifically crescent leg raises, hip rotations and the dynamic hamstring scoop stretch, are highly beneficial for improving performance in the turning kick. Crescent leg raises help to activate and mobilise the hip flexors and adductors, crucial for the chambering and extension phases of the kick. The outward and inward sweeping motion mimics the arc trajectory of the turning kick, ensuring the hips are warmed up for dynamic movement. Hip rotations promote flexibility and mobility in the hip joint, which is essential for achieving the correct pivot and alignment during the kick. Meanwhile, the dynamic hamstring scoop stretch enhances hamstring flexibility, reducing the risk of injury and supporting the high extension required for an effective turning kick. Together, these stretches prepare the lower body for the demands of the technique, promoting fluidity, control, and power in execution.

By incorporating these dynamic stretches into your warm-up routine, you'll prepare your body for the dynamic movements involved in executing a turning kick, ensuring optimal performance and reduced risk of injury.

## CORRECT TECHNIQUE AND BIOMECHANICAL PRINCIPLES

The turning kick is a fundamental technique in various martial arts disciplines. Its biomechanics involve intricate movements of the entire body, combining coordination, balance and strength to generate power. Below is an overview of the biomechanics involved in executing a roundhouse kick.

1. **Stance and preparation** Start in a stable fighting stance, typically with one foot forward and the other foot pivoted to provide balance and mobility. The arms are often used for balance and defence, with one arm guarding the face and the other extending outwards to maintain distance from the opponent.
2. **Chambering and initiation** The kicking leg is initially chambered, with the knee raised towards the side of the chest and the foot flexed to provide power and speed during the kick. The hips play a crucial role in initiating the kick. They rotate explosively towards the target, generating torque and momentum that will be transferred into the kick.

**Lateral leg swings** The initial phase of the lateral leg swing begins with a stable stance. The standing leg's foot is already turned out to ensure smooth movement. Lift the swinging leg out to the side, keeping the hips square and the core engaged. Maintaining balance is key during this phase to prepare for the full swing. Keep your posture upright and your arms in a steady position for support if needed. This phase sets the foundation for controlled, fluid leg swings.

In the lateral leg swing's active phase, the leg moves in a wide arc across the body and out to the side. Ensure the hips, shoulders and heel of the swinging leg remain aligned throughout the motion. The swing should be fluid and controlled, avoiding jerky movements. Gradually increase the height of each swing, focusing on dynamic flexibility. Perform ten to fifteen swings per leg.

Knee lifts with rotation enhance core strength, flexibility and hip mobility. Begin by standing upright with feet hip-width apart and arms extended to the sides. Lift one knee toward your chest while rotating your torso towards the raised knee. Hold for a moment before lowering the leg. Alternate sides, performing ten to twelve repetitions per leg to engage the hip flexors and obliques effectively.

3. **Extension and impact** As the hips rotate, extend the kicking leg towards the target. Keep the leg straight and tense, with the foot positioned to strike with the instep or ball. The point of impact varies depending on the target and your preference. Common targets include the torso, head or legs of the opponent.
4. **Follow-through and recoil** After making contact with the target, the kicking leg continues its trajectory, ensuring maximum force is transferred into the strike. Following the kick, quickly recoil the leg back to its chambered position, ready to defend or execute additional techniques if necessary.

### Biomechanical Principles

The turning kick utilises several biomechanical principles to optimise power and efficiency. These include:

- **Rotation** The rotation of the hips generates angular momentum, which is transferred into the kick to increase its speed and force.
- **Acceleration** The kicking leg accelerates rapidly as it extends towards the target.
- **Deceleration** After impact, the leg decelerates to prevent overextension and maintain balance.
- **Counter-rotation** The upper body may counter-rotate in the opposite direction of the kick to enhance stability and balance.
- **Muscle activation** Muscles throughout the body, including the core, hips and legs, work synergistically to execute the kick with power and precision.

Understanding the biomechanics of the turning kick is essential for martial artists to optimise their technique, improve performance and minimise the risk of injury. Through proper training, conditioning and biomechanical analysis, practitioners can refine their turning kick to be a formidable weapon in sparring scenarios.

## PERFECTING THE TURNING KICK IN ITF PATTERNS

In Taekwon-Do patterns, the turning kick must demonstrate proper technique, power, precision and a correct trajectory to score well with umpires. The kick travels in a smooth arc and must break at the appropriate stopping angles to show control and accuracy. In ITF patterns, the middle turning kick stops at a 45-degree angle and targets the shoulder level, while the high turning kick stops at a 25-degree angle and attacks at eye level. The low turning kick targets the umbilicus level. Delivering the kick with balance, control and a strong recoil highlights technical correctness and improves scoring potential.

## EXAMPLES OF INCORRECT TECHNIQUE

Incorrect technique in the turning kick can diminish its effectiveness and leave you vulnerable to counter-attacks. Here are common mistakes to avoid:

- **Telegraphing the kick** Signalling the kick prematurely by dropping the guard or making other movements that alert the opponent allows them to anticipate and counter effectively.
- **Insufficient chambering** Failing to raise the knee high enough towards the chest during the initial phase of the kick results in reduced power and reach. Proper chambering is essential for generating maximum force and maintaining control over the kick's direction.
- **Incorrect trajectory** Executing the kick along an incorrect path, either too high or too low from the intended target area, leads to diminished power and accuracy. Ensuring the correct angle is crucial for striking the target effectively.
- **Incorrect foot shape** Failing to maintain the proper foot shape upon impact, for example not pointing the toes for sparring or flexing the foot to produce the ball of the foot for

power breaking, results in less effective strikes and increased risk of injury. Proper foot positioning ensures maximum impact and safety.

- **Weak execution** Not putting enough power into the kick reduces its impact and effectiveness in a power-breaking or sparring scenario, compromising your ability to control the situation. Strong hip rotation and full-body engagement are necessary for a powerful kick.
- **Overextending the leg** Fully extending the leg too early in the kicking motion leaves it vulnerable to being blocked or countered, and reduces power and control. Proper timing of the extension is essential to maintain power and stability.
- **Incomplete rechamber** Failing to swiftly bring the leg back to the starting position after extending the kick leaves you exposed to counter-attacks and compromises balance and safety. Quick rechambering also aids in maintaining a defensive posture.
- **Leaning backwards** Shifting the body's weight away from the target by leaning backwards during the kick reduces the effectiveness, power and stability of the strike, and allows for loss of balance. Maintaining a forward lean helps keep the centre of gravity aligned with the target, enhancing your stability and power.
- **Inadequate hip rotation** Fully pivoting on the standing foot and rotating the hips during the kick are essential for generating maximum power. Proper hip rotation helps in transferring the body's momentum into the kick, making it more effective.
- **Lack of follow-through** Stopping the kick short instead of following through with the motion reduces the force and impact. A complete follow-through ensures the kick delivers maximum power and keeps the opponent on the defensive.

This turning kick demonstrates significant errors that compromise both technique and effectiveness. The standing leg shows no pivot, which is essential for allowing the hips to open and align correctly with the kicking motion. Without this pivot, the hips remain closed, causing the kicking leg to struggle to achieve the proper foot shape. The ball of the foot is pointing upwards instead of being parallel to the floor, preventing the correct striking surface from making contact at a 90-degree angle with the target. This incorrect alignment affects the trajectory of the kick, meaning the ball of the foot would not strike with optimal force or accuracy. The lack of pivot also limits hip rotation and reduces overall balance, power generation and control, all of which are crucial for an effective turning kick. Proper pivoting of the standing foot is essential to ensure the kicking leg can extend with correct trajectory, alignment and foot shape for maximum impact.

By avoiding these common mistakes, you can ensure your turning kick is powerful, accurate, and effective, enhancing your overall performance in sparring and self-defence situations.

### Incorrect Foot Shapes

- **Pointed toes** Keeping the toes pointed during the turning kick rather than kicking with the ball of the foot is not only an incorrect foot shape but also a dangerous one, as there is a high risk of injury.
- **Skewed foot** Positioning the kicking foot in a skewed or incorrect position, for example pressing the ball of the foot upwards instead of parallel to the floor, can compromise the accuracy and power of the kick and could cause injury.
- **Unbalanced standing foot** Failing to pivot the standing foot and maintain balance upon landing the Turning Kick can lead to instability, making it difficult to execute follow-up or consecutive techniques and leaving the practitioner vulnerable to counterattacks.

In Taekwon-Do, understanding the correct technique is essential for maximising the power, speed and precision of each turning kick while minimising the risk of injury. Proper training and attention to detail are crucial. Practitioners can improve their turning kick technique by asking their instructor for corrections or by filming their technique and critiquing themselves. This helps in identifying and correcting common mistakes, leading to optimal performance.

## BASIC STRENGTH, MOBILITY AND CONDITIONING EXERCISES

Enhance the effectiveness of your turning kick with targeted exercises that build the muscles essential for rotation, stability, and power generation. Prioritise a thorough warm-up and consider consulting with a personal trainer to ensure proper form and technique.

To optimise your turning kick, focus on strengthening the muscles involved in rotation and stability. Here are key exercises to incorporate into your regimen, grouped by muscle groups and with instructions for each.

## Lower Body Strength Exercises

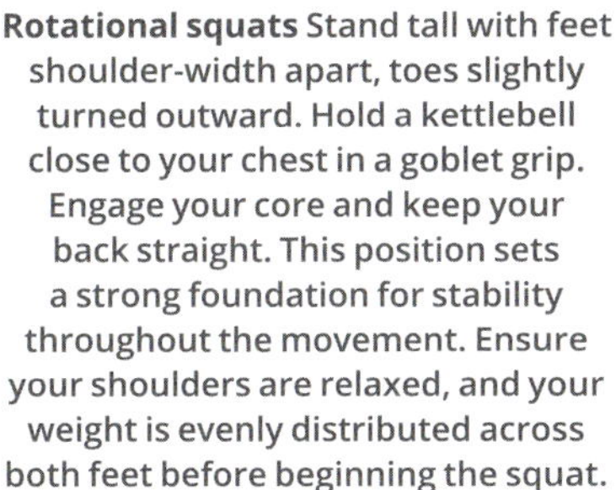

**Rotational squats** Stand tall with feet shoulder-width apart, toes slightly turned outward. Hold a kettlebell close to your chest in a goblet grip. Engage your core and keep your back straight. This position sets a strong foundation for stability throughout the movement. Ensure your shoulders are relaxed, and your weight is evenly distributed across both feet before beginning the squat.

Lower into a deep squat by bending your knees and pushing your hips back as if sitting into a chair. Keep your chest lifted and core engaged to maintain good posture. Ensure your knees track over your toes, avoiding inward collapse. Your thighs should be parallel to the floor at the squat's lowest point, holding the kettlebell steady.

While maintaining the squat position, rotate your torso to one side, keeping your core tight and the kettlebell close to your chest. The movement should come from your hips and core, not just the shoulders. Return to the centre, stand back up, and repeat the squat, rotating to the opposite side. Perform ten to twelve reps on each side for balanced strength development.

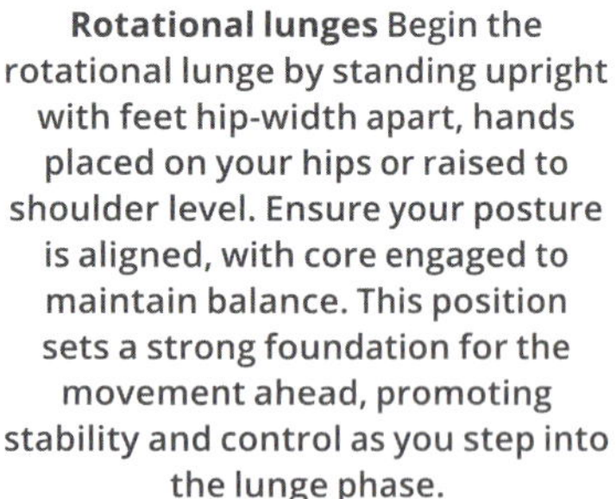

**Rotational lunges** Begin the rotational lunge by standing upright with feet hip-width apart, hands placed on your hips or raised to shoulder level. Ensure your posture is aligned, with core engaged to maintain balance. This position sets a strong foundation for the movement ahead, promoting stability and control as you step into the lunge phase.

Take a long step forward with your right leg, bending both knees to lower into a lunge. Keep your chest lifted and core tight. As you descend, rotate your torso towards your leading leg, engaging your obliques for a dynamic twist. Maintain balance by distributing weight evenly between the legs, avoiding any forward lean.

Push through your right heel to rise back to the standing position, ensuring you maintain control throughout the movement. Alternate to the left side by stepping forward with your left foot and rotating your torso in the same manner. Perform ten to twelve reps on each side, focusing on fluid and controlled transitions between each repetition.

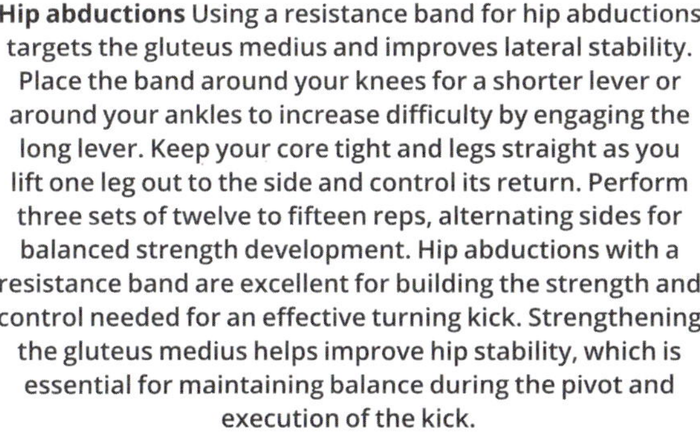

**Hip abductions** Using a resistance band for hip abductions targets the gluteus medius and improves lateral stability. Place the band around your knees for a shorter lever or around your ankles to increase difficulty by engaging the long lever. Keep your core tight and legs straight as you lift one leg out to the side and control its return. Perform three sets of twelve to fifteen reps, alternating sides for balanced strength development. Hip abductions with a resistance band are excellent for building the strength and control needed for an effective turning kick. Strengthening the gluteus medius helps improve hip stability, which is essential for maintaining balance during the pivot and execution of the kick.

**Weighted chamber lifts** These help build strength and endurance in the hip flexors, quads and core, which are all crucial for an effective turning kick. Holding a weight along the leg during the lift increases resistance, enhancing muscle engagement. This drill improves your ability to hold a high chamber position, ensuring a strong and controlled kick execution. Perform three sets of ten to twelve reps per side for optimal results. Weighted lifts develop the necessary strength to lift and hold the leg in a high position, improving balance and control during the kick. This exercise also mimics the chamber phase of the turning kick, reinforcing proper alignment and muscle building for a more effective and efficient strike.

**Bicycle crunches** These target the obliques and strengthen the core, essential for maintaining balance and control during kicks. Keeping your shoulders off the ground, rotate your torso to bring the opposite elbow toward the knee in a pedalling motion. This movement improves rotational strength, which enhances your turning kick technique. Perform three sets of twelve to fifteen reps on each side.

**Plank position** The plank is essential for developing core stability and strengthening the muscles that support powerful kicks. This position demonstrates correct form, with a straight line from the head to the heels and engaged core muscles. Maintaining this alignment helps improve balance and control in techniques like turning kicks, ensuring efficient energy transfer from the core to the leg.

**Plank rotation** Plank rotations enhance core engagement and develop rotational strength, which is crucial for kicks that require body twisting, like turning kicks. This exercise involves starting in a plank position, then rotating the torso to lift one arm towards the ceiling, engaging the obliques and stabilising muscles. The movement improves balance, stability and coordination. Perform three sets of ten to twelve reps on each side, focusing on smooth and controlled transitions to mimic the pivoting action needed during kicks, enhancing precision and fluidity in technique execution.

## POWER TESTING WITH THE TURNING KICK

When practising the turning kick on a kickshield, maximising power requires proper technique, body mechanics, and targeting. Here's how to kick a kickshield with optimal power:

### Power Testing with a Kickshield

1. **Stance and distance** Start by assuming the appropriate stance. Stand with your feet shoulder-width apart, with the kickshield positioned in front of you at a comfortable distance. Ensure you're in a stable and balanced stance before initiating the kick.
2. **Chambering** Begin the turning kick by chambering your kicking leg. Lift your knee up towards your chest while keeping your foot flexed and your shin parallel to the ground. This chambering position allows you to generate maximum power when extending your leg.
3. **Rotation** Initiate the kick by rotating your body. Pivot on the supporting foot while turning your hips and shoulders towards the target (the kickshield). This rotation generates torque and momentum, which will amplify the power of your kick.
4. **Extension** As you rotate, extend your kicking leg towards the kickshield. Aim to make contact with the target using the instep or ball of your foot, depending on your preference and training style. Fully extend your leg, keeping it straight and tense throughout the movement.
5. **Impact** Make contact with the kickshield with a snapping motion. This snapping action adds speed and force to your kick, increasing its impact on the target. Focus on striking the kickshield with the intended part of your foot, aiming for the centre or slightly off-centre to maximise power.
6. **Follow-through** After making contact with the kickshield, follow through with your kick. Continue the kicking motion past the target, allowing your leg to fully extend and your body to rotate back to its starting position. This follow-through ensures that you transfer maximum force into the kick.
7. **Breathing** Coordinate your breathing with the execution of the kick. Inhale as you chamber your leg and exhale forcefully as you extend it towards the kickshield. This controlled breathing helps to enhance the power and focus of your kick.
8. **Repeat and practise** Repeat the turning kick on the kickshield multiple times to develop 'muscle memory' and refine your technique. Focus on maintaining proper form, generating maximum power with each kick, and adjusting your technique as needed.
9. **Feedback and correction** Seek feedback from a qualified instructor or training partner to identify areas for improvement. They can provide guidance on refining your technique, adjusting your body mechanics and increasing power output.
10. **Gradual progression** Gradually increase the intensity and speed of your kicks as you become more proficient. Start with slow, controlled movements and gradually ramp up the power and speed as your technique improves.

### Power Breaking

Once you have trained your turning kick on the kickshield, you can move onto breaking boards with the kick, also known as power breaking, which requires precise technique, proper execution, and sufficient power. Below is a step-by-step guide on how to power break boards with a turning kick:

1. **Select the right boards** Choose boards appropriate for your skill level and strength. Typically, thin wooden boards of pine are used for beginner to intermediate levels, while thicker

boards or multiple boards are used for advanced practitioners.

2. **Warm up** Warm up your body thoroughly to prevent injuries. Perform dynamic stretches and practise your turning kick technique to prepare your muscles and joints for the breaking.
3. **Positioning** Position the boards securely on a solid surface, such as a sturdy stand or between two supports. Ensure that the boards are aligned properly and there's enough space for your kicking technique.
4. **Focus on technique** Focus on proper technique throughout the entire kick. Begin by assuming the appropriate stance, with your feet shoulder-width apart and your body facing the target. Chamber your kicking leg by bending your knee and lifting it towards your chest.
5. **Generate power** Generate power by rotating your body explosively. Rotate your hips and pivot on the supporting foot as you extend your kicking leg towards the target. The power in your turning kick comes from the rotation of the hips and the speed at which your leg travels.
6. **Strike the target** Aim to strike the boards with the ball of your foot. Focus on hitting the boards with a snapping motion, concentrating force on a small area to break through cleanly.
7. **Follow through** Follow through with your kick completely to ensure maximum force and penetration. Your kicking leg should continue its trajectory past the boards, driving through the target.
8. **Maintain balance** Maintain your balance and stability throughout the kick. Keep your core engaged and your body centred over your supporting leg to prevent falling or stumbling after the break.
9. **Practise safely** Practise power breaking under the supervision of a qualified instructor, especially if you are a beginner. Use proper protective gear, such as hand and foot pads, or board padding to minimise the risk of injury.
10. **Progress gradually** Start with thinner boards and gradually increase the thickness or number of boards as you gain confidence and strength. Focus on improving your technique and power with each attempt.
11. **Evaluate and adjust** After each attempt, evaluate your performance and adjust your technique as needed. Pay attention to areas where you may be lacking in power or accuracy and make necessary corrections in your training.
12. **Consistent practice** Power breaking requires consistent practice to develop the necessary strength, conditioning,

Power breaking with a turning kick requires precision, power and accuracy. Begin by aligning your stance, pivoting your supporting foot, and rotating your hips to generate force. Strike the board with the ball of your foot, focusing on a clean, powerful impact. Depending on the flexibility of your toes and your ability to present the ball of the foot as the striking tool, you may need to adjust the angle at which you kick. This adjustment ensures the correct trajectory for your body, maximising force while reducing the risk of injury. Gradually progress to thicker boards as your strength, technique and accuracy improve.

speed and technique. Incorporate board-breaking drills into your training regimen regularly to improve your skills over time.

By following these steps and practising diligently, you can develop the ability to power break boards with a turning kick effectively. Remember to prioritise safety, proper technique and gradual progression in your training.

## STATIC STRETCHING ROUTINE FOR TURNING KICKS

Preparing your body for the demands of martial arts, particularly executing powerful turning kicks, requires flexibility and mobility in key muscle groups. This static stretching routine is designed to target specific areas such as the adductors, piriformis, medial glutes, hamstrings and spine

**Adductor and hamstring stretch** Sit on the floor with legs extended wide in a straddle position. Lean from the hips, reaching towards your right foot to feel a stretch along your left inner thigh. Hold for 20–30 seconds, ensuring your torso stays aligned. Repeat on the left side. This stretch enhances flexibility for kicks by improving hip mobility and reducing injury risk. Perform two to three sets per side.

**Piriformis stretch** Sit on the floor with your left leg extended in front and your right leg bent. Cross your right foot over your left thigh, placing it flat on the floor. Use your hands to brace and gently pull your left leg closer to your torso. Hold for 20–30 seconds, feeling the stretch in your glutes. Switch sides and repeat for two to three sets per leg.

**Wall-assisted medial glute stretch** Lie on your back with your left foot resting against a wall, knee bent at 90 degrees. Cross your right ankle over your left thigh to form a figure-four position. Press gently into your right knee to deepen the stretch or bring your foot further down the wall closer to you. Hold for 20–30 seconds, feeling the stretch in your right glute. Switch sides and perform two to three sets.

**Single-leg hamstring stretch** Sit on the floor with your right leg extended and your left foot resting against your inner thigh. Keep your back straight as you lean forward from your hips, reaching towards your right foot. Feel the stretch along the back of your right thigh. Hold for 20–30 seconds, then switch sides. Perform two to three sets per leg.

**Thread the needle stretch (spine rotation)** Begin in a tabletop position with hands and knees on the floor. Reach your right arm underneath your left arm and leg, lowering your right shoulder and cheek to the ground. Feel the stretch along your spine and shoulder. Hold for 20–30 seconds. Switch sides and repeat. Perform two to three sets per side for improved flexibility.

rotation to optimise your roundhouse kick performance. By incorporating these stretches into your training regimen, you can enhance your flexibility, reduce the risk of injury and improve your overall martial arts technique.

Remember to breathe deeply and maintain proper form throughout each stretch.

## KEY ELEMENTS COVERED IN THIS CHAPTER

- The turning kick's versatility in targeting opponents from various angles and heights
- The importance of the chamber, extension, and rechamber (CER) sequence for optimal power and precision
- Initiation and execution of the kick involving coordinated body mechanics and engagement of core muscles
- Principles and techniques for precise execution, including targeting, foot positioning and maintaining visibility of the arms
- Rear leg, lead leg and double variations of the turning kick, each offering unique advantages and challenges
- Engagement of specific muscle groups essential for executing a powerful and precise turning kick
- Dynamic stretching and mobility routine to prepare the body for turning kick practice
- Correct technique guidelines and common mistakes to avoid in executing the turning kick
- Exercises to enhance strength, mobility and conditioning, targeting muscles involved in rotation and stability
- Guidelines for power testing with the turning kick on a kickshield and power breaking with boards.
- Static stretching routine targeting key muscle groups to optimise roundhouse kick performance

## LOOKING AHEAD

In the next chapter, we will delve into the mechanics, applications and training methods for executing the downward kick, providing practitioners with a comprehensive understanding of this technique.

# 10 THE DOWNWARD KICK

The downward kick, *naeryo chagi* in Korean, is a fundamental technique in Taekwon-Do, recognised for its powerful and direct approach. In this chapter, we will explore the nuances of this kick, covering its essential components and more advanced variations, providing you with the skills necessary to perform it accurately with maximum impact and control.

It's worth noting that a similar kick, the axe kick, shares some mechanics with the downward kick. However, the axe kick is not included in the ITF Taekwon-Do Encyclopaedia, although there is a similar that is – the straight kick *(jigeau chagi)*, where both legs are straight while kicking and the back heel is used as the striking tool. For the sake of this book, we will look at downward kick and the axe kick.

## DOWNWARD KICK

The downward kick is designed to strike an opponent from above, and is executed by lifting the leg high into the chamber position and forcefully driving the heel down towards the target. This kick begins by lifting the knee high, with the leg bent, positioning the foot above the intended target. The leg is then extended swiftly, driving the heel downwards in a powerful motion, with force generated primarily from the hips and lower body. The point of focus for this kick should not be lower than the attacker's solar plexus, as targeting below this point can result in a loss of power.

A downward kick executed with control and force – striking from above with the heel or sole to target the opponent's head, shoulder or collarbone. This technique relies on flexibility, timing and precision, delivering powerful impact through a vertical arc.

The skull is the main target, with the clavicle as a secondary target. This kick also arcs broadly across the body to clear obstacles before striking the target. After striking, the leg is retracted back to the original stance or prepared for the next move in a sequence. The downward kick involves the engagement of the hip flexors and the core to ensure a controlled and powerful descent, with a vertical trajectory to maximise impact force.

Both the downward kick and the axe kick utilise the heel as their primary striking tool, though the ball of the foot can also be employed in variations of the axe kick during sparring.

## AXE KICK

The axe kick, although not included in the condensed Taekwon-Do Encyclopaedia, is a similar technique with a distinctive arcing motion. This kick starts by lifting the leg high, with little to no bend or chamber, preparing to strike downwards. At the peak of the arc, the leg is fully extended, with the heel leading the motion as it descends onto the target. The axe kick typically aims for the head, shoulder or collarbone, engaging the hamstrings and hip flexors to ensure a fluid and forceful motion. After the strike, the leg is brought back to the original stance or readied for the next move.

## STRIKING TOOLS

### Downward Kick

The primary striking tool for the downward kick is the heel. This kick involves driving the heel straight down with significant force generated from the hip and core muscles. The heel is particularly effective when targeting hard structures such as the skull and clavicle, as its density allows for a concentrated and forceful impact.

### MUSCLES ENGAGED IN A DOWNWARD OR AXE KICK

| Muscle group | Function |
|---|---|
| **Quadriceps** | Primary extension of the knee joint, responsible for straightening the leg during the kick |
| **Hamstrings** | Assist in hip extension and knee flexion, crucial for generating power and control in the kick |
| **Gluteus maximus** | Primary hip extensor, driving forceful movement of the leg backward |
| **Hip flexors** | Facilitate lifting the leg into the chamber position, initiating the kicking motion |
| **Core muscles** | Provide stability and control throughout the kick, transferring power from the lower body to foot |
| **Gastrocnemius** | Plantar flexes the foot, contributing to the extension of the lower leg during the kick |
| **Soleus** | Assists the gastrocnemius in plantar flexion, aiding in pushing off the ground |

### Axe Kick

Similarly, the axe kick predominantly uses the heel as the striking tool. As the leg reaches the peak of its arc, the heel is brought down onto the target. This motion leverages gravity to augment the force delivered, making the heel an optimal choice for maximising impact on the head, shoulder or collarbone. The ball of the foot is generally not used in the axe kick, as the nature of the kick requires a strong and durable point of impact to ensure both effectiveness and safety. However, during sparring, a practitioner may use the ball or the underside of the foot to gain some extra distance.

Dynamic stretches such as front leg raises increase blood flow to the muscles, enhance flexibility and improve joint mobility, ensuring your body is primed for the movements required in executing downward or axe kicks in Taekwon-Do.

## MUSCLES USED IN A DOWNWARD KICK

Executing a downward or an axe kick in Taekwon-Do requires precise coordination and strength, engaging various muscle groups throughout the body. The effectiveness of these kicks depends not only on technique but also on the power and control derived from specific muscles. The following table outlines the primary muscle groups involved in performing these powerful and dynamic kicks, highlighting their roles in generating force, stability and accuracy.

### Dynamic Stretching and Mobility Routine

Before practising the downward or axe kick in Taekwon-Do, it's essential to warm up your muscles with dynamic stretches targeting key areas like the hamstrings and hip flexors. These stretches prepare your body for the dynamic motions involved in kicking while reducing the risk of injury.

Dynamic stretching plays a key role in improving flexibility and mobility for downward and axe kicks by preparing the muscles and joints for explosive movements. Key stretches include hamstring scoops to loosen the hamstrings, hip circles to improve hip mobility, and leg swings to enhance dynamic range. Leg crescents target hip control and lateral movement, while runner lunges and kneeling hip flexor stretches focus on stretching the hip flexors and promoting balance. Finally, knee raises activate the hip flexors and improve control during upward leg movements. The step-by-step instructions for these stretches have been outlined in previous chapters.

## CORRECT TECHNIQUE AND BIOMECHANICAL PRINCIPLES

Performing a downward or axe kick in Taekwon-Do requires precise technique and an understanding of biomechanical principles to generate maximum power and effectiveness. Below is a breakdown of the biomechanics involved in executing these kicks.

**The downward/axe kick** The downward and axe kicks begin with a balanced stance, ensuring stability on the supporting leg. Shift your weight slightly to the base leg, engaging the core for control. The chambering motion lifts the kicking leg across the body, engaging the hip flexors. This setup is essential for creating momentum and maintaining balance before extending the leg into the kick.

As the kicking leg transitions from chamber to extension, the quadriceps power the movement, driving the foot upward before the downward motion. For both kicks, the leg follows a controlled arc. Hip flexion and knee extension work in unison to deliver the striking foot toward the target. Maintaining core engagement ensures balance and control during this explosive phase of the kick.

After the kick reaches its target, the leg is quickly retracted to maintain control and balance. The rechambering motion prevents the kicker from being off-guard post-strike. The foot returns to its original position, preparing for follow-up techniques. Precision in the end phase ensures that the kick maintains power while allowing the practitioner to maintain balance and readiness for further movements.

1. **Stance and initiation** Start in a balanced stance, shifting weight to the supporting leg for stability.
2. **Chambering** Lift the kicking leg with a bent knee for a downward kick or a straighter leg for an axe kick, engaging the hip flexors.
3. **Extension** Extend the leg rapidly, driving the foot downward for a downward kick or in an arc for an axe kick, powered by the quadriceps.
4. **Foot positioning** Adjust the foot to strike with the heel or ball, ensuring control and precision on impact.
5. **Hip action** Use hip flexion and extension to drive the leg's motion, generating power and reach.
6. **Trunk rotation** Slight trunk rotation can add torque, increasing power, especially when aiming high.
7. **Balance and stability** Keep the core engaged and the supporting leg steady to prevent excessive sway.
8. **Breathing** Exhale forcefully at impact to enhance focus and power output.
9. **Follow-through** After impact, retract the leg or prepare for the next move while maintaining balance.

Understanding the biomechanics of the downward or axe kick enables practitioners to refine their technique, improve efficiency, and maximise the effectiveness of their kicks. By focusing on proper body mechanics and incorporating specific training drills, martial artists can enhance their kicking capabilities and excel in combat situations. Remember to adhere to the foot positioning guidelines outlined in Taekwon-Do Encyclopaedia for formal patterns, although the downward kick only appears in Tong-Il Tul, while adapting footwork for sparring or bag work to optimise thrust and power.

## COMMON MISTAKES AND INCORRECT TECHNIQUE

- **Insufficient chambering** Failing to lift the knee high enough reduces the potential power and trajectory of the kick.
- **Improper foot positioning** Striking with the wrong part of the foot, for example with the toes instead of the heel, leads to decreased impact and potential injury.
- **Poor hip engagement** Neglecting to engage the hips limits the force and downward momentum of the kick.
- **Lack of core stability** Weak or unengaged core muscles result in loss of balance and reduced control during the motion.
- **Overextending the supporting leg** Straightening the supporting leg excessively compromises balance and stability.
- **Incorrect targeting** Aiming too low (below the solar plexus) reduces effectiveness and wastes the downward trajectory's power.
- **Flat trajectory** Allowing the leg to descend in a shallow arc rather than a steep vertical motion weakens the impact.
- **Failure to retract** Not returning the kicking leg to the chamber position after striking leaves the practitioner vulnerable.
- **Excessive upper body movement** Leaning too far back or to the side destabilises the stance and reduces control.
- **Breathing errors** Holding the breath or exhaling too early reduces focus and power during execution.

## BASIC STRENGTH, MOBILITY AND CONDITIONING EXERCISES

To enhance the power and strength of your downward or axe kick, it's crucial to incorporate exercises that target the key muscle groups involved in the kicking motion. A comprehensive strength and conditioning routine will focus on improving the strength, stability and flexibility of these muscles.

Squats, lunges, Romanian deadlifts, and calf raises target the lower body, improving strength and stability in the quadriceps, gluteus maximus, hamstrings, and calves. Core stability exercises, such as planks and Russian twists, are crucial for maintaining balance, posture and rotational power. Each exercise has been detailed in previous chapters with step-by-step instructions to ensure correct technique and maximise effectiveness, along with recommended sets and repetitions to build a strong, resilient body.

### Upper Body Strength Exercises

Investing time in your upper body conditioning is crucial for improving the posture and strength of your downward/axe kick. Here are some basic upper body exercises to incorporate into your training programme.

Incorporate these exercises into your training routine to improve the power, stability and effectiveness of your downward or axe kick. Start with manageable weights and focus on proper form to prevent injury. Consistency and progressive overload are key for continual improvement in strength and power for martial arts techniques like the downward or axe kick. If possible, consult a personal trainer to tailor a specific programme of strength and conditioning training for your needs and goals.

**Dumbbell shoulder press** This exercise targets your deltoid muscles for improved shoulder strength and stability. Seated or standing, hold dumbbells at shoulder height and press them overhead until your arms are fully extended. Lower them back with control. Perform three sets of eight to ten reps. This exercise enhances balance and core strength, supporting powerful strikes and defensive movements in martial arts.

**Push-ups** The push-up begins in a high plank position, engaging your core for stability. Place your hands slightly wider than shoulder-width apart and ensure your body forms a straight line from head to toe. This initial position sets the foundation for proper push-up technique, targeting the deltoids, core muscles, and chest.

As you lower your body towards the ground, maintain a straight alignment and control your movement. Keep your elbows at a 45-degree angle, lowering your chest to nearly touch the floor. This phase works your deltoids and core, promoting strength and endurance. Focus on a slow, controlled descent to maximise muscle engagement before pressing back up to the starting position. Perform three sets of eight to twelve reps for optimal strength-building.

**Quadriceps stretch** Improve your kicking power and flexibility by stretching your quadriceps. Stand upright, bringing one heel towards your buttocks, and hold your ankle or foot with your hand. Keep your knees aligned and push your hips slightly forward to deepen the stretch. Hold this position for 20–30 seconds, maintaining balance and control. Perform two to three sets on each leg to enhance mobility, stability and overall leg strength for martial arts techniques.

**Groin stretch (butterfly stretch)** This stretch helps improve hip mobility and flexibility, essential for effective kicking techniques. Sit on the floor with the soles of your feet together and your knees naturally falling to the sides. Hold your feet with your hands, keeping your back straight, and gently press your knees down to deepen the stretch. Hold for 20–30 seconds, repeating for two to three sets to enhance your range of motion and reduce tension in the groin muscles.

**90/90 hip stretch** This stretch is perfect for improving hip flexibility, essential for strong kicking techniques. Begin in a kneeling position with your front knee bent at a 90-degree angle and your back leg extended behind you at the same angle. Keep your torso upright, engage your core, and shift your hips into a posterior pelvic tilt to increase the stretch. Hold for 20–30 seconds, repeating two to three sets on each leg to release tension and improve mobility.

## Static Stretching for Flexibility

A static stretching routine is crucial for improving flexibility and range of motion, both of which are essential for executing downward or axe kicks effectively and safely. Stretches such as the hamstring stretch, low lunge stretch, adductor stretch and calf stretch are all effective in improving flexibility and mobility required for executing the downward or axe kick with control and range. These exercises target key muscle groups involved in the kick, including the hamstrings, hip flexors, adductors and calves, helping to reduce the risk of injury and enhance performance. While these stretches have been covered in detail in previous chapters, the following exercises offer valuable additions to any static stretching programme for martial arts kicking techniques.

Performing each stretch for two to three sets allows for a more thorough stretching routine, promoting flexibility and preventing muscle tightness. Concentrate on breathing deeply and relaxing into each stretch, gradually increasing the intensity as your muscles loosen up. Incorporate this static stretching routine into your warm-up and cool-down routine before and after practising downward or axe kicks to enhance flexibility and reduce the risk of injury.

## KEY ELEMENTS COVERED IN THIS CHAPTER

- Understanding the proper chambering, extension and retraction of the kicking leg, crucial for generating power and precision in downward and axe kicks
- Exploring the differences between the downward kick, targeting the skull, clavicle

or face, and the axe kick, which arcs broadly across the body before striking the target

- Recognising common mistakes in technique, such as insufficient chambering or incorrect foot positioning, and providing guidance on how to correct these errors to optimise kick performance
- Incorporating strength and conditioning exercises that target key muscle groups involved in executing downward and axe kicks, including the quadriceps, hamstrings, hip flexors, gluteus maximus, core muscles, deltoids and calf muscles
- Implementing static stretching routines to improve flexibility and range of motion, crucial for executing downward and axe kicks with proper form and reducing the risk of injury

## LOOKING AHEAD

In the next chapter, we will delve into the side kick, building upon the foundations established in mastering the downward and axe kicks. Side kicks offer unique challenges and opportunities, expanding the practitioner's arsenal of striking techniques.

An axe kick delivered with height and precision, lifting vertically before driving down with force through the heel. This powerful technique targets the head or collarbone, combining flexibility, control and timing to break guard and disrupt balance from above.

# 11 THE SIDE KICK

The side kick, *yop chagi* in Korean, is a fundamental technique in Taekwon-Do, celebrated for its power, precision and versatility. This kick can target an opponent to the side or the front, making it a highly adaptable kick in both offensive and defensive situations. Capable of attacking low, middle and high targets, the side kick is typically executed from a chambered position, allowing for a direct and forceful strike using the blade of the foot.

In sparring, the side kick can be delivered from either the rear or the lead leg, with each variation offering distinct advantages in terms of speed, reach and impact.

In this chapter, we will explore the technical aspects of the side kick, including its proper execution, common variations and practical applications. Through detailed analysis and step-by-step guidance, you will gain a deeper understanding of this essential technique, enhancing your overall Taekwon-Do skill set.

A side kick performed with precision and intent: the body aligned, the foot sword extended and the hips driving through the target. This technique delivers maximum power along a straight line, combining balance, control and explosive force to stop an opponent in their tracks.

## FUNDAMENTAL ELEMENTS

The side kick in Taekwon-Do requires precision, balance and power. To execute it effectively, several key principles must be observed. Firstly, the attacking tool, which is the footsword, must reach the target in a straight line accompanied by a revolving motion of the hip and body. This straight-line path ensures efficiency and speed, while the revolving motion adds power and stability to the kick.

**The side kick** The side kick starts with a solid chamber. Position the kicking foot near the inner knee joint of the stationary leg to enhance balance and control. Keep your toes pointed slightly downwards, and ensure your supporting foot faces outward at around a 75-degree angle. This preparation phase sets up a powerful, precise kick.

During the extension phase of the side kick, drive your footsword straight out towards the target with full hip rotation. Maintain balance by keeping the supporting foot angled outward in a full pivot and engaging your core. The toes of the kicking foot should point slightly downward to ensure correct alignment, delivering power and accuracy to the strike.

After impact, return to the rechamber position to maintain balance and reset your stance. Rechambering stops you leaving your leg extended, which could compromise stability and expose you to counter-attacks. Proper rechambering ensures control over your kicking technique, allowing you to recover quickly and prepare for the next move.

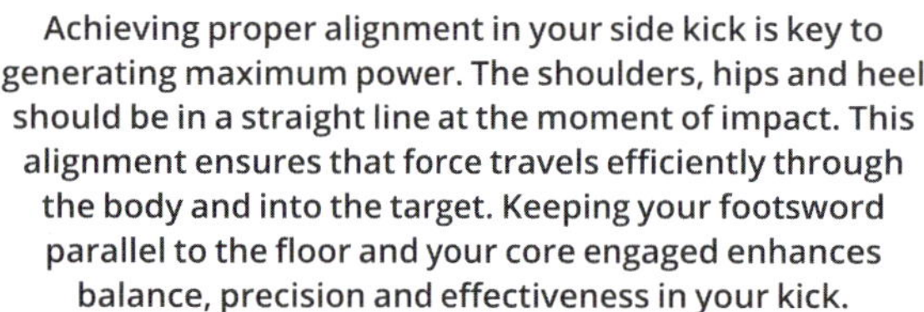

Achieving proper alignment in your side kick is key to generating maximum power. The shoulders, hips and heel should be in a straight line at the moment of impact. This alignment ensures that force travels efficiently through the body and into the target. Keeping your footsword parallel to the floor and your core engaged enhances balance, precision and effectiveness in your kick.

A common mistake is the 'bananaed' side kick. The hips are not properly engaged, causing the kick to follow a diagonal arc. Notice the bottom sticking out and the torso dipping downward. This incorrect posture reduces the kick's power and precision, as the force is dissipated. To avoid this, keep your hips aligned and engage your core for a straight, powerful trajectory.

For achieving maximum height, it is important to lean the body away from the direction of the kick as far as possible while still maintaining balance. This counterbalance helps extend the reach and height of the kick without compromising stability. Additionally, it is essential to avoid kicking diagonally, as this dissipates the force of the kick – don't stick your bottom out and perform the kick in a banana shape. A straight-line delivery focuses all the generated power directly into the target, maximising the impact.

Unless otherwise instructed by an instructor or the Taekwon-Do Encyclopaedia, executing a high punch with the same-side fist as the kicking foot (so right fist with right foot) is required for ITF Taekwon-Do line work and in several of the patterns. This simultaneous action not only adds to overall coordination but also helps with balance and power generation. Middle side kicks in patterns have to be executed at shoulder height, and high kicks to eye height.

Lastly, the stationary foot must pivot to allow the hip to rotate with the kick. This pivoting motion is critical as it facilitates the full range of motion for the hip, generating greater power and ensuring proper alignment of the body during the kick.

## TYPES OF SIDE KICK

In Taekwon-Do, the side kick can be executed in various forms, each with its unique characteristics and applications. The primary variations are the side piercing kick, side pushing kick, and side thrusting kick. Understanding the differences between these kicks is essential for effectively employing them in different scenarios.

Each side kick variation serves a distinct purpose within Taekwon-Do. The side piercing kick is ideal for precise, powerful strikes to vulnerable areas. The side thrusting kick allows the practitioner to maintain distance while delivering forceful impacts. The side pushing kick is useful for controlling and manipulating the opponent's position with less emphasis on causing injury. Understanding and practising these variations enables practitioners to adapt their techniques to different combat scenarios effectively.

The side piercing kick is one of the most effective techniques for attacking an opponent from the flank. This kick uses the footsword as the attacking tool and targets vulnerable areas such as the temple, armpit, floating ribs and neck artery. Secondary targets include the philtrum, point of the chin and solar plexus. The side piercing kick can be executed at low, middle and high levels, making it versatile for various situations. The precision and power of this kick come from its ability to strike in a direct and focused manner, delivering significant force to the targeted area.

The side thrusting kick is a variation of the side piercing kick, with the primary difference being its ability to attack the front of the opponent's body from a distance. This kick employs the ball of the foot as the attacking tool, which reaches the target in a straight line with minimal revolving motion. At the moment of impact, the ball of the foot should be vertical to the target with the ankle stretched. This technique allows for greater reach and can be effective in situations where maintaining distance from the opponent is advantageous. When wearing shoes, the toes can also be used for this kick.

## Side Pushing Kick

The side pushing kick *(yopcha milgi)* is a variation of the side piercing kick, but it relies on weight and mass rather than acceleration and power. Consequently, it lacks the piercing force of other side kicks, and the rapid withdrawal of the kicking foot is less critical. The footsword is the only attacking tool used in this technique. The side pushing kick is typically executed from sitting, diagonal or parallel stances. During execution, it is important to cross the other foot rapidly past the position where the kicking foot has been placed, ensuring the target is pushed momentarily. This kick is effective for creating space and controlling an opponent's position without necessarily inflicting significant damage.

**The side pushing kick** In the sitting stance start position, ensure your shoulders, hips and feet are aligned, creating a stable base for the side pushing kick. This stance enhances balance and allows the transfer of weight into the pushing action. Maintain focus on your target, keeping your hands ready to guard. Proper positioning here sets the foundation for effective execution of the technique.

During the side pushing kick, begin by stepping the supporting foot behind the kicking leg's starting position. This positioning enhances stability and maximises the pushing force directed at the target. As you shift your weight, prepare the footsword by chambering the kicking leg. Ensuring precision in this stage allows for a smooth, controlled execution, crucial for displacing an opponent without compromising your own balance.

The execution phase of the side pushing kick focuses on driving the footsword into the target with a controlled, pushing motion. Unlike a piercing kick, this technique relies on mass and steady pressure rather than speed. Keep your kicking leg extended briefly to push the opponent back, then retract calmly. This technique is highly effective for creating space and managing an opponent's movement.

## COMPARING SIDE KICK VARIATIONS

| | Side piercing kick | Side thrusting kick | Side pushing kick |
|---|---|---|---|
| **Primary attacking tool** | Footsword | Ball of the foot | Footsword |
| **Target areas** | Temple, armpit, floating ribs, neck artery, philtrum, chin solar plexus | Front of the opponent's body | Varies; primarily for pushing and controlling |
| **Path to target** | Direct and focused | Straight line with minimal revolving | Cross step footwork is used to direct weight and mass efficiently, focusing more on control and positioning rather than acceleration |
| **Stance used** | Various | Various | Sitting, diagonal, parallel |
| **Impact characteristics** | High piercing force, rapid withdrawal | Impact with ankle stretched to produce the ball of the foot | Pushing force, less emphasis on rapid withdrawal |
| **Body position at impact** | Ankle positioned for footsword strike | Ball of the foot vertical to the target | Ankle positioned for footsword strike |
| **Application** | Effective for precise, powerful strikes | Maintains distance, delivers concentrated impacts | Controls opponent's position, creates space |

## KEY STRIKING POINTS FOR THE TAEKWON-DO SIDE KICK

| Key striking point | Description |
|---|---|
| **Solar plexus** | Located just below the sternum, this is a central and vulnerable spot on the torso, delivering a strike here can cause significant pain and disrupt breathing |
| **Ribs** | Targeting the ribs can cause significant discomfort and potential damage, affecting the opponent's ability to breathe and move |
| **Abdomen** | Aiming for the abdomen can wind the opponent and disrupt their balance |
| **Floating ribs** | These are the lower ribs that are not attached to the sternum, making them more susceptible to damage |
| **Thigh (quadriceps)** | In self-defence, aiming at the thigh can cause muscle injury, limiting the opponent's mobility |
| **Knee** | In self-defence, striking the knee can cause joint damage, significantly hindering the opponent's movement and stability |
| **Head (jaw or temple)** | A high side kick aimed at the head can be very effective, potentially knocking out the opponent or causing severe disorientation. In sparring, controlled kicks to the head score the most points |
| **Chest (pectoral muscle)** | Aiming at the chest can knock the wind out of the opponent and push them back, creating distance. In sparring controlled kicks to the torso score points |
| **Shoulder** | A well-placed kick to the shoulder can affect the opponent's arm movement and balance, which could be a tactical use during sparring |

## STRIKING POINTS

These striking points are selected based on their vulnerability and the potential impact a well-executed side kick can have on an opponent. Proper targeting can maximise the effectiveness of the side kick in both sparring and self-defence situations.

## MUSCLES USED IN THE SIDE KICK

The side kick in Taekwon-Do engages several major muscle groups, each playing a critical role in executing the technique effectively. Understanding these muscle groups can help practitioners enhance their performance and prevent injury through targeted strength training and stretching exercises.

By training these muscle groups, Taekwon-Do practitioners can improve their strength, flexibility and overall effectiveness in executing side kicks. Regular conditioning and stretching of these muscles is also essential for injury prevention and enhancing the power and accuracy of the kick.

### Dynamic Stretching and Mobility Routine

Prepare for powerful side kicks with the dynamic stretching routine below. Designed to enhance flexibility and mobility, these exercises are essential for preventing injury and maximising performance in Taekwon-Do.

Dynamic exercises such as leg swings, hip circles, lunges with torso twist, leg raises, hip flexor stretches and dynamic hamstring scoop stretches are excellent for preparing the body for the side kick. These movements target the muscles and joints involved in the kick, promoting flexibility, mobility and control while reducing the risk of injury. All these exercises have been covered in previous chapters, highlighting their importance in dynamic warm-ups for martial artists. The exercise shown here is another effective addition to a dynamic warm-up programme for martial artists looking to enhance their kicking performance.

### MUSCLES ENGAGED IN A SIDE KICK

| Muscle group | Primary muscles | Function in side kick |
|---|---|---|
| **Hip flexors** | Iliopsoas (psoas major, iliacus) | Lift the knee and chamber the leg |
| **Hip extensors** | Gluteus maximus | Extend the hip during the kick |
| **Quadriceps** | Rectus femoris, vastus lateralis, vastus medialis, vastus intermedius | Extend the knee |
| **Hamstrings** | Biceps femoris, semitendinosus, semimembranosus | Control leg movement, assists in retraction |
| **Adductors** | Adductor longus, adductor brevis, adductor magnus | Stabilise the leg, maintain balance |
| **Abductors** | Gluteus medius, gluteus minimus | Lift the leg sideways, stabilise the pelvis |
| **Core muscles** | Rectus abdominis, obliques (internal and external), transverse abdominis | Maintain balance and stability, transfer power |
| **Calves** | Gastrocnemius, soleus | Stabilise the supporting leg, ensure proper foot positioning |
| **Erector spinae** | Spinalis, longissimus, iliocostalis | Maintain upright posture and balance |

**Dynamic side kicks** Begin in a balanced stance, ensuring your posture is stable and your hands are in guard position. Slowly extend your leg into a side kick, focusing on correct alignment, hip engagement and the footsword as your striking tool. Gradually increase the speed and height of each kick as your muscles warm up. Perform ten to twelve dynamic side kicks on each leg to improve flexibility, control and kicking power.

In ITF Taekwon-Do patterns, there are various positions that the hands must be in while performing the kick. Unless stated otherwise in the Taekwon-Do Encyclopaedia, the arms should be in a punch position with the fist at eye level. When chambering the kick, gather your hands in front of your chest and punch out as you extend the kick.

## CORRECT TECHNIQUE AND BIOMECHANICAL PRINCIPLES

The side piercing kick is a fundamental technique in Taekwon-Do, requiring precise biomechanical movements to deliver powerful strikes to specific targets. Below is a breakdown of the biomechanics involved in this kick.

1. **Stance and preparation** Begin in a balanced stance, with one foot forward and the other positioned slightly back for stability. The arms are typically used for balance and defence, with one arm guarding the face and the other extending outwards to maintain distance from the opponent.
2. **Chambering and initiation** The kicking leg is chambered, with the knee raised towards the side of the chest and the foot positioned to strike with the footsword. The hips play a crucial role in initiating the kick, rotating explosively towards the target to generate torque and momentum.
3. **Extension and impact** As the hips rotate, extend the kicking leg towards the target in a straight line, with the footsword aimed at specific vulnerable areas such as the temple, armpit, floating ribs or neck artery. The footsword makes contact with the target with precision and power, delivering a piercing force that can incapacitate the opponent.
4. **Follow-through and recoil** After making contact with the target, the kicking leg continues its trajectory, ensuring maximum force is transferred into the strike. Following the kick, quickly recoil the leg back to its chambered position, ready to defend or execute additional techniques if necessary.

## Biomechanical Principles

The side piercing kick utilises several biomechanical principles to optimise power and efficiency:

- **Rotation** The rotation of the hips generates angular momentum, which is transferred into the kick to increase its speed and force.
- **Extension** The kicking leg extends in a straight line towards the target, maximising the reach and impact of the kick.
- **Muscle activation** Muscles throughout the body, including the core, hips and legs, work synergistically to execute the kick with power and precision.

Understanding the biomechanics of the side piercing kick is essential for Taekwon-Do practitioners to optimise their technique, improve performance and deliver effective strikes in sparring or self-defence situations. Through consistent training and biomechanical analysis, practitioners can refine their side piercing kick to be a formidable weapon in their martial arts arsenal.

## Striking Tools

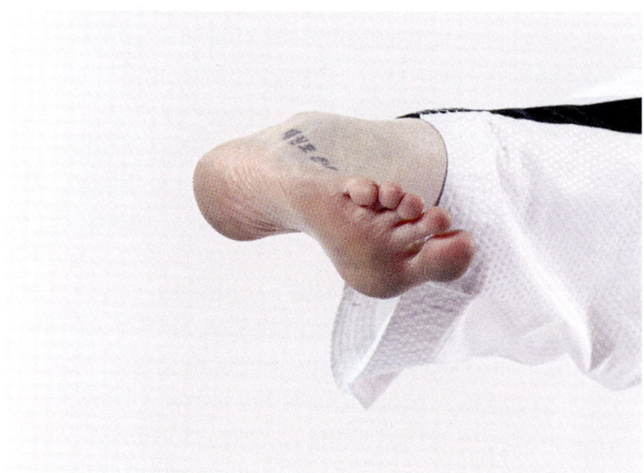

The footsword is the primary striking tool for side kicks, including both side piercing and side pushing kicks. The toes should be angled slightly downwards, keeping the heel higher to ensure proper alignment. This foot shape allows for a precise strike, maximising power transfer into the target while maintaining balance and control. Ensuring the correct foot position is essential for effective execution and reducing injury risk.

The ball of the foot is the correct striking tool for the side thrusting kick. To ensure maximum impact, the toes should be flexed upward, keeping the ball of the foot firmly aligned with the target. This striking surface allows for a focused and penetrating thrust, delivering powerful force while maintaining stability and control during the kick execution.

# COMMON MISTAKES AND INCORRECT TECHNIQUE

**Poor chambering** In this side kick, the knee is not lifted high enough or drawn across and close to the chest, which compromises the kick's precision and power. Proper chambering ensures control, balance and a direct kicking trajectory. Without a high knee lift, the kick loses its linear force and becomes less effective, impacting both speed and impact on the target.

**Over- or under-rotation of the hips** The power and stability of a side kick depend heavily on the correct rotation of the hips. Over-rotating causes the kick to swing wide and lose force, while under-rotating limits reach and power. To maximise the impact, the hips must align with the kicking foot, ensuring balance and directing the force straight into the target.

**Incorrect foot shape and pivot issues** This side kick highlights several common errors. The toes are pointing up instead of down, exposing the sole rather than the footsword, resulting in a weak and ineffective striking tool. Additionally, the lack of a proper pivot on the supporting foot limits hip rotation, compromising the correct trajectory and reducing both power and balance. Correcting these elements is essential for an effective, stable and precise side kick.

- **Leaning too far** Overcompensating by leaning excessively backward or sideways compromises balance.
- **Lack of core engagement** Weak or unengaged core muscles result in a lack of balance and reduced force.
- **Dropping the guard** Allowing arms to drop instead of maintaining a defensive position leaves openings for counters.
- **Failure to recoil** Not retracting the kicking leg after the strike leaves the practitioner exposed.
- **Improper breathing** Holding the breath or exhaling at the wrong moment reduces focus and power.
- **Targeting errors** Aiming at overly low or incorrect areas reduces the kick's effectiveness and exposes vulnerabilities.

## BASIC STRENGTH, MOBILITY AND CONDITIONING EXERCISES

To enhance the power and effectiveness of your side kick, it's essential to incorporate exercises that target the key muscle groups involved in executing this technique. A well-rounded strength and conditioning routine will focus on improving strength, stability and flexibility in these areas. The exercises listed below target specific muscle group.

### Lower Body Strength Exercises

The previously outlined strength and conditioning exercises, such as squats, lunges, Romanian deadlifts and calf raises, are highly effective in building the key muscles involved in executing a strong and controlled side kick. These exercises target the quadriceps, hamstrings, gluteus maximus, hip flexors and calf muscles, helping to improve power, balance and stability, which are essential for this technique. The exercises shown here provide further options to strengthen the side kick by focusing on lower-body strength and overall kicking performance.

## LOWER BODY STRENGTH EXERCISES

**Wall side kick rotations** This is a powerful exercise to improve your side kick stability and core strength. Begin by placing your foot up against the wall in a side kick position. Hold a weight at chest level for added resistance. Keep your body as upright as possible and maintain balance throughout. This position simulates the precise control needed for a strong side kick.

The next step involves rotating your torso from side to side. This movement targets the oblique muscles, which are essential for maintaining the correct body alignment in a side kick. Proper engagement of the obliques ensures stability, balance and power during the kick. Perform three sets of twelve to fifteen reps on each leg to strengthen your core and enhance your kicking technique.

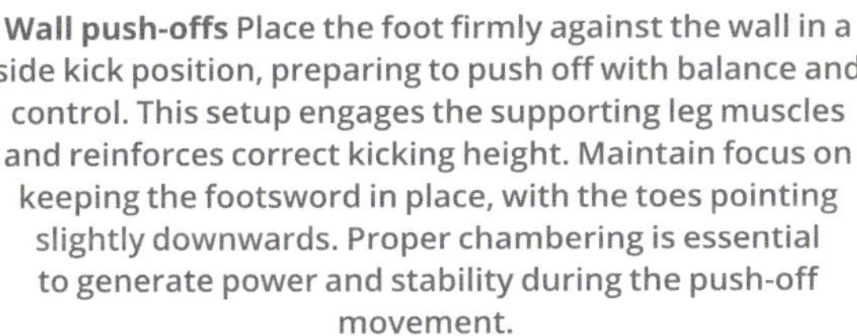

**Wall push-offs** Place the foot firmly against the wall in a side kick position, preparing to push off with balance and control. This setup engages the supporting leg muscles and reinforces correct kicking height. Maintain focus on keeping the footsword in place, with the toes pointing slightly downwards. Proper chambering is essential to generate power and stability during the push-off movement.

Executing the push-off from the wall while maintaining the chambered position enhances balance, stability and strength. As you push back from the wall, focus on keeping your kicking leg at the same height throughout the movement. The hop back to the wall should be controlled, with the foot returning to the original position to complete each repetition. Perform three sets of twelve to fifteen reps on each leg for effective results.

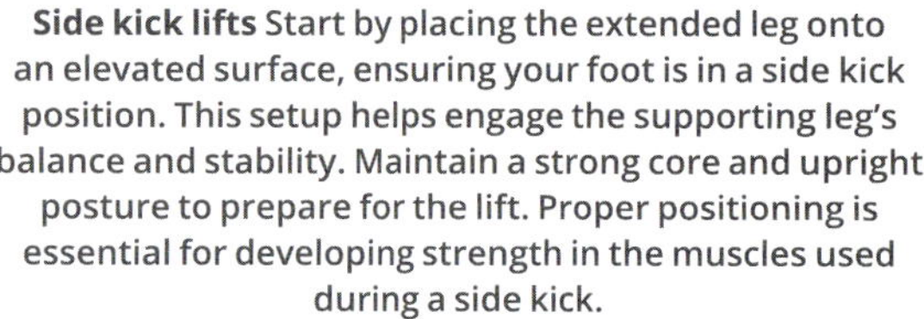

**Side kick lifts** Start by placing the extended leg onto an elevated surface, ensuring your foot is in a side kick position. This setup helps engage the supporting leg's balance and stability. Maintain a strong core and upright posture to prepare for the lift. Proper positioning is essential for developing strength in the muscles used during a side kick.

From the resting position, lift your leg off the surface into a controlled side kick position. Hold for five seconds to strengthen the hip flexors, glutes and core. Slowly lower your leg back to the surface, maintaining control throughout. Perform three sets of twelve to fifteen reps on each leg to improve your technique and muscle endurance.

**Side kick with a resistance band** Begin by looping a resistance band around your foot and holding the ends securely with both hands. Take a solid stance, either with support from a wall or without for an advanced version. Position your leg into a side kick chamber, ensuring your balance is stable. This setup prepares you to activate the muscles needed for controlled side kick extension.

Press your leg into a full side kick extension against the resistance of the band. Focus on engaging your glutes and hips to maintain stability while the band offers resistance. Hold the extended position for five seconds before smoothly returning to the chamber. Perform three sets of twelve to fifteen reps on each leg to build strength and control in your kicks.

# STATIC STRETCHING FOR FLEXIBILITY

A static stretching routine is essential for improving flexibility and range of motion, which are crucial for executing powerful, high and precise side kicks.

**Forward folding groin stretch** Sit on the floor with the soles of your feet together and your knees relaxed, falling out to the sides. Hold your feet with both hands, gently pressing your knees towards the ground. Slowly lean forward, bringing your chest down and aiming to touch your head towards or onto your feet. Hold this stretch for 20–30 seconds and repeat for two to three sets to enhance flexibility.

**Adductor stretch** Sit on the floor in a straddle position with your legs extended as wide as comfortable. Slowly walk your hands forward, lowering your chest towards the floor while keeping your back straight. Ensure your hips remain squared to the front to engage the adductor muscles effectively. Hold the stretch for 20–30 seconds, focusing on deepening it with each exhale. Repeat for two to three sets to improve flexibility.

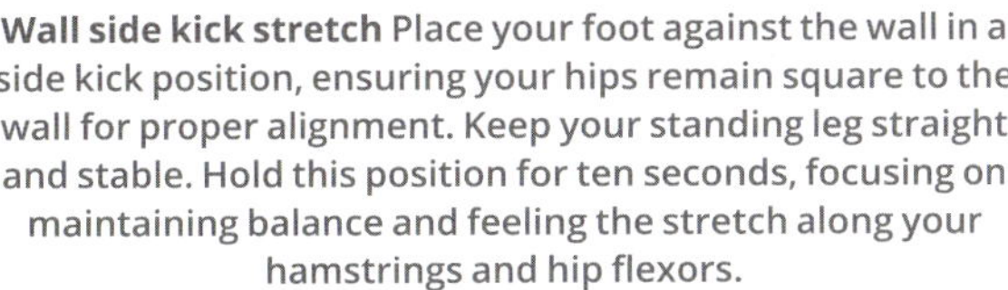

**Wall side kick stretch** Place your foot against the wall in a side kick position, ensuring your hips remain square to the wall for proper alignment. Keep your standing leg straight and stable. Hold this position for ten seconds, focusing on maintaining balance and feeling the stretch along your hamstrings and hip flexors.

From the initial side kick position, slowly bend forward to stretch towards your standing leg, deepening the stretch. Maintain a straight back and keep your foot pressed against the wall. Hold this stretch for ten seconds before returning to the upright position. Gradually inch your leg higher up the wall to intensify the stretch. Perform two to three sets on each leg.

**Wall straddle split** This stretch targets the inner thighs and hip flexibility. Lie on your back with your legs elevated against the wall in a straddle position, allowing gravity to aid in deepening the stretch. Keep your back flat and relax into the position. Hold for one to two minutes, gradually increasing duration as flexibility improves. Perform two to three sets, ensuring a controlled release.

Incorporating these exercises into your training routine will help improve the power, stability and effectiveness of your side kick. Focus on proper form and gradually increase the intensity to continue challenging your muscles. Consult with a personal trainer if needed to tailor a specific programme to your needs and goals.

### Static Stretching for Flexibility

The previously outlined static stretches, such as the hamstring stretch, calf stretch, quadriceps stretch, and low lunge stretch, are valuable for improving flexibility and mobility in the key muscle groups required for an effective side kick. These stretches target the hamstrings, quadriceps and hip flexors, helping to reduce the risk of injury while enhancing range of motion and control. The exercises shown here provide additional static stretches that can further improve flexibility for side kick performance.

Performing each stretch for two to three sets allows for a thorough stretching routine, promoting flexibility and preventing muscle tightness. Remember to breathe deeply and relax into each stretch, gradually increasing the intensity as your muscles loosen up. Incorporate this static stretching routine into your warm-up and cool-down before and after practising side kicks to enhance flexibility and reduce the risk of injury.

## POWER BREAKING WITH THE SIDE KICK

Start in a side-facing stance with your weight evenly distributed and your front leg prepared to kick. To generate more power and momentum, step your rear leg behind the kicking leg in a step-up motion. As you chamber the kick by lifting your knee high and keeping your heel aimed at the target, rotate your hips and pivot on your supporting foot to drive force into the strike. Focus on striking with the footsword, but more towards the heel of your foot, keeping your toes pulled back to maximise the impact on the board. Visualise your kick penetrating through the board and follow through completely, allowing your leg to continue its motion past the target. Maintain balance and control throughout the movement, resetting your stance quickly if needed. The key to a successful break is combining speed, precision, and full-body coordination to transfer maximum energy into the board.

## KEY ELEMENTS COVERED IN THIS CHAPTER

- Understanding the fundamental principles of the side kick, including proper chambering, extension and retraction of the kicking leg, essential for generating power and accuracy
- The key variations of the side kick – the side piercing kick, side pushing kick and side thrusting kick – each with its unique characteristics and applications
- Recognising the biomechanical principles behind the execution of the side kick, including hip rotation, foot positioning and body alignment, to maximise effectiveness and minimise the risk of injury
- Exploring strength and conditioning exercises tailored to target the muscle groups involved in executing the side kick, such as the quadriceps, hamstrings, hip flexors, gluteus maximus, core muscles and calf muscles
- Implementing static stretching routines aimed at improving flexibility and range of motion, crucial for executing side kicks with proper form and reducing the risk of injury

## LOOKING AHEAD

Next we will start delving into intermediate kicks, starting with the hooking kick, to further expand your repertoire of striking techniques, providing new challenges and opportunities for growth in your Taekwon-Do practice.

Power breaking with the side kick requires precision, alignment and explosive force.

# 12 | THE HOOKING KICK

The hooking kick, *golcho chagi* in Korean, is a sophisticated defensive technique in Taekwon-Do, designed to counter or redirect an opponent's attack. This chapter delves into the technique, exploring its execution, variations and the biomechanical principles that underpin its effectiveness.

A defensive hooking kick in action, expertly parrying the opponent's punch off-line while maintaining balance and readiness. This technique showcases timing, spatial awareness and precision, using the sole or instep to redirect the attack and create an immediate counter-attacking opportunity. A smart blend of defence and control.

## TYPES OF HOOKING KICK

### In Defence

The hooking kick is primarily a defensive manoeuvre, employed to block or redirect incoming attacks. The technique is executed by using the side instep of the kicking foot, which approaches the target with an outward curve. This curvature helps in both deflecting the opponent's attack and positioning the foot for a potential counter-attack.

The hooking kick can be executed at low or middle levels, depending on the height of the incoming attack and the intended target. The effectiveness of the kick lies in its ability to redirect attacks while positioning the practitioner for an immediate counter.

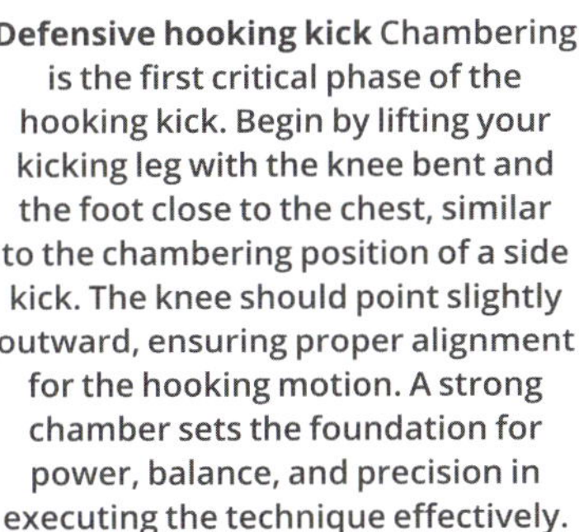

**Defensive hooking kick** Chambering is the first critical phase of the hooking kick. Begin by lifting your kicking leg with the knee bent and the foot close to the chest, similar to the chambering position of a side kick. The knee should point slightly outward, ensuring proper alignment for the hooking motion. A strong chamber sets the foundation for power, balance, and precision in executing the technique effectively.

The extension phase involves pushing the leg outward in a controlled motion. Aim the side instep toward the target while ensuring a smooth curve in the movement. The kick should be executed with precision and power, ready to deflect an incoming attack or strike effectively. Maintain balance and posture throughout.

After delivering the kick, the leg must be quickly rechambered to prepare for the next move. Retract the leg back to the chest, maintaining control and balance. The rechambering phase ensures readiness for a follow-up attack or to return to a defensive stance, keeping the opponent on edge.

The hooking kick shown in action, effectively deflecting an incoming punch. The hooking motion of this kick allows the practitioner to block or redirect the opponent's strike, creating an opportunity for a counter-attack. Ensure proper foot shape and hip rotation to maximise the kick's deflective capability.

The follow-up counter-attack using a powerful side kick aimed at the opponent. The practitioner delivers the kick with precision and control, targeting the opponent's torso. This smooth transition from defence to offence is what makes the hooking kick so effective when combined with a decisive counter, maintaining control of the engagement while keeping the opponent off-balance.

## In Offence

The offensive hooking kick is a distinct yet related technique. Unlike the hooking kick, which is primarily defensive, this kick is designed to strike with a hooking motion.

**Offensive hooking kick** Begin by lifting the kicking leg, keeping the knee high and bent towards the chest. The chambered position should angle the knee outward slightly. Ensure the supporting leg is stable and pivoted to allow for smooth rotation. This high chamber is essential for both balance and the initial setup of the hooking kick's trajectory.

Extend the leg outwards in a near-straight motion towards the target. The toes should point slightly outwards as the kick follows a curved path. To maximise the effectiveness, whip the leg back in a hooking motion. This sweeping movement is designed to catch the opponent from an unexpected angle, improving the kick's impact.

After making contact with the target using the heel or sole of the foot, quickly retract the leg to its chambered position. The hooking effect should be smooth yet controlled to maintain balance and prepare for follow-up techniques. Swift rechambering ensures you remain in control and ready to counter-attack or reposition as needed.

A high offensive hooking kick executed with precision, targeting the opponent's temple using the ball of the foot. The kick demonstrates excellent control and flexibility, with the practitioner maintaining a stable base while delivering a swift, curved strike. This technique is effective for catching the opponent off-guard, aiming for a critical target to maximise impact and disrupt their balance.

## COMPARING HOOKING KICK VARIATIONS

| | **Hooking kick** | **Offensive hooking kick** |
|---|---|---|
| **Purpose** | Defensive kick used to block or redirect an incoming attack | Offensive kick used to strike the target with a hooking motion |
| **Execution** | Delivered with the side instep in an outward curve | Performed with the kicking foot's heel slightly off-target, then whipped back to strike |
| **Target area** | Outside of the attacking hand or foot | Head |
| **Striking tool** | Outward curve of the side instep | Bottom of the heel, back of the heel or flat sole of the foot |
| **Knee position at impact** | Tibia of the kicking leg facing downward | Knee bends (snaps) before impact for a hooking finish |
| **Chambering** | Chambering not specific; focuses on defensive placement | Chambered similarly to a side kick with an added hooking motion at the end |
| **Leg position at impact** | Leg may be nearly straight at impact | Leg can be nearly straight or hooked with a bent knee |
| **Kick height** | Delivered low or middle | Can be delivered high, middle or low |
| **Follow-through** | Often retracted for a counter-attack or returned to stance | Whipped back to continue striking or retract for follow-up |
| **Application in patterns** | Executed in Juche move 7 and 19 | Used in pattern and sparring, for example in high, hooking motions or slow motion reverse hooking kicks in patterns such as Juche |

## In Offence

The offensive hooking kick *(huryeo chagi)* can be aimed with a straight leg or with a hooked finish, depending on the desired effect. This kick is versatile and can be used to strike from different angles, catching the opponent off-guard.

# THE USE OF HOOKING KICKS IN ITF PATTERN JUCHE

The ITF Taekwon-Do pattern Juche incorporates a variety of kicking techniques, among which the hooking kicks play a significant role. Specifically, the pattern features two types of hooking kick: the reverse hooking kick *(bandae dollyo goro chagi)* and the hooking kick *(golcho chagi)*.

In the pattern, hooking kicks serve both defensive and offensive purposes. The reverse hooking kick is used with a spinning motion to deliver powerful, surprise attacks, while the hooking kick acts as a defensive tool that transitions smoothly into subsequent offensive moves. Learning these kicks enhances the practitioner's ability to execute complex patterns with precision and effectiveness, highlighting the integrated nature of Taekwon-Do techniques within pattern training.

## Reverse Hooking Kick

In Juche, the reverse hooking kick is executed in slow motion during moves 5 and 17. A high reverse hooking kick is used that strikes with the heel; it bears resemblance to the offensive hooking kick but includes a spinning element.

*Execution and Application*

- **Chambering and execution** The kick begins with a high chambered position. The leg is drawn back with the knee bent, and as the kick is executed, it involves a full spin. This creates a powerful rotational force, driving the heel of the kicking foot towards the target.
- **Impact point** The heel is the primary striking surface, similar to the offensive Hooking Kick, but the spinning motion adds a dynamic element, making it a potent offensive technique.
- **Strategic use** The slow-motion execution in Juche emphasises control and precision. This high reverse hooking kick can be utilised to intercept or counter an opponent's attack from a high angle, leveraging the spinning motion to increase the impact force and surprise the opponent.

## Hooking Kick

The hooking kick appears in moves 7 and 19 of Juche, executed prior to a consecutive high side piercing kick (*see* Part 2, Chapter 4). This application of the hooking kick is crucial for transitioning between techniques and maintaining the flow of the pattern.

*Execution and Application*

- **Chambering and execution** The hooking kick involves a side instep strike, where the kicking leg curves outward to block or redirect an incoming attack. The kick is performed at a mid-level height, targeting the outside of the opponent's hand or foot.
- **Impact point** The side instep is used to make contact with the target. The kicking leg's tibia should be facing downwards at the moment of impact to ensure effective deflection and control.
- **Strategic use** The hooking kick is primarily a defensive move, used to neutralise an opponent's attack. Its placement before a high side piercing kick allows the practitioner to quickly transition from defence to offence, creating a seamless flow in the pattern. This combination of techniques is designed to maintain momentum and exploit openings in the opponent's defence.

A poor foot shape for hooking kick, where the foot is turned too far outwards.

# COMMON MISTAKES AND INCORRECT TECHNIQUE

## Hooking Kick

Common mistakes primarily involve improper chambering, poor foot shape and lack of control in the kick's arc.

- **Insufficient chambering** Practitioners often fail to lift the knee high enough or neglect to angle the leg outward correctly, which disrupts the intended sweeping arc of the kick.
- **Incorrect foot alignment** The foot is frequently misaligned, with some striking too high on the ankle instead of using the appropriate part of the outer tibia for effective deflection.
- **Dropping the guard** During execution, this exposes the practitioner to counterattacks.
- **Incorrect body alignment** Leaning too far forwards or backwards, or failing to rotate the hips, compromises both balance and power.
- **Incorrect trajectory** A trajectory that is too flat or straight, lacking the required curved motion, and insufficient core engagement further contribute to balance loss and reduced control.
- **Targeting errors** Aiming too low reduces the kick's tactical effectiveness, while incorrect timing can render the kick ineffective in both offensive and defensive scenarios.

## Offensive Hooking Kick

- **Improper chambering** Chambering at the wrong angle limits the hooking effect essential to the kick's success.
- **Incorrect foot shape** Striking with incorrect parts of the foot – such as the ankle or ball of the foot – rather than the heel, back of the heel or sole, diminishes the kick's impact and increases the risk of injury.

- **Arcing problems** Lack of control in the arc results in jerky, uneven motions that reduce fluidity and power, while overextending the leg or creating an excessively wide arc makes the kick slow and predictable.
- **Incorrect body alignment** Failing to rotate the hips sufficiently, in particular, results in a loss of torque and power.
- **Incomplete rechamber** Neglecting to whip the leg back properly during rechambering diminishes the follow-through and leaves the practitioner vulnerable.
- **Incorrect trajectory** A flat trajectory, as opposed to the intended curved motion, detracts from the technique's effectiveness.
- **Weak core** A poorly engaged core leads to a lack of balance and control.
- **Targeting errors** Missing high or lateral targets reduces the tactical value of the kick, and incorrect timing – either premature or delayed – limits its utility in various combat scenarios.

## DYNAMIC STRETCHING AND MOBILITY ROUTINE

To effectively prepare for the dynamic and powerful hooking kicks in Taekwon-Do, it is crucial to warm up and enhance flexibility in the muscles and joints involved. This routine focuses on increasing range of motion, improving muscle activation, and reducing the risk of injury.

These dynamic stretches and mobility exercises are designed to activate and loosen the muscles and joints involved in executing hooking kicks. They will improve your kicking technique by enhancing flexibility, coordination and overall range of motion.

This image highlights common errors when performing the offensive hooking kick. The supporting foot lacks proper pivot, limiting hip rotation and reducing balance. The foot shape of the kicking leg is incorrect, with the toes pointing upward instead of the heel leading the motion. The body alignment is off, affecting both the power and accuracy of the kick.

**Hip flexor and hamstring kick-throughs** This exercise targets both the hip flexors and hamstrings while improving flexibility and control. Begin by standing with your feet hip-width apart. Lift one leg straight in front of you, maintaining a fully extended position. Smoothly swing the leg out to the side, then bring it across your body to aim for your opposite hand. Perform eight to ten kick-throughs on each leg for an effective dynamic stretch.

**Leg swings** Start by standing upright with your feet shoulder-width apart. For balance, you may hold onto a stable surface if needed. Swing one leg straight forward in a controlled manner. Gradually increase the height of the swing as you go, aiming to keep your body posture upright. Forward leg swings help to loosen the hip flexors and improve dynamic flexibility.

After completing the forward swing, transition smoothly into the backward swing. The backward motion should be equally controlled, ensuring your leg moves in a straight line. Avoid arching your back or bending your knee. Backward leg swings are essential for warming up the glutes and hamstrings, preparing the body for powerful kicking techniques. Perform ten to fifteen swings per leg for best results.

**Standing glute stretch** Begin by standing upright with your feet hip-width apart. Cross your right ankle over your left knee to form a figure-four shape. Keep your back straight and your core engaged to maintain balance. Place your hands on your hips or keep them in front of you for added stability.

Slowly lower your hips toward the ground, as if sitting into a squat. Ensure your back stays straight and your chest remains lifted. You should feel a stretch in your right glute and hip. Hold this position for a few seconds before standing back up. Perform eight to ten repetitions on each leg, keeping the movement controlled and steady.

**Dynamic high knees** Start in a standing position with your feet hip-width apart. Lift one knee towards your chest while driving the opposite arm forward, as if mimicking a sprinting motion. Quickly alternate legs in a controlled running movement, focusing on lifting your knees as high as possible. Engage your core throughout the exercise to maintain stability and balance. This movement helps improve cardiovascular endurance, coordination and leg strength. Aim to perform 20–30 high knees on each leg for an effective workout.

**Quadriceps stretch** Begin by standing upright with your feet hip-width apart. Bend your right knee, bringing your heel toward your glutes. Hold your ankle with your right hand to keep your balance and gently pull your foot closer to increase the stretch in your quadriceps. Keep your chest lifted and your core engaged to maintain stability.

**Knee drive** From the quadriceps stretch position, gently lean forward while maintaining the grip on your ankle. Drive your bent knee slightly forward to deepen the stretch through the hip flexor and quadriceps. Focus on a controlled movement, ensuring your back stays straight and you maintain balance. Hold the knee drive for a few seconds before returning to the upright position. Repeat eight to ten times on each leg.

## BASIC STRENGTH, MOBILITY AND CONDITIONING EXERCISES

To enhance the effectiveness and power of your hooking kicks, it's important to incorporate exercises that build strength, stability and flexibility in the key muscle groups involved. Shown here are exercises targeting these areas, which are essential for executing powerful and precise hooking kicks.

### Static Stretching for Flexibility

Static stretching is essential for improving flexibility and range of motion, both of which are crucial for executing effective hooking kicks. By following the step-by-step instructions for the stretching exercises outlined in the previous chapters, you can incorporate these stretches into your warm-up or cool-down routine to maximise your training results. Key stretches, including hamstring, quadriceps, hip flexor, adductor, calf and groin

**Banded offensive hooking kicks** Begin in a side kick position, extending your foot into a secure resistance band. Hold the band firmly in both hands to maintain tension. Keep your supporting leg slightly bent and engage your core to stabilise the movement. This exercise helps build control, strength and balance, focusing on the glutes and hamstrings for an effective hooking kick.

From the extended side kick position, smoothly hook your foot toward your bottom, while maintaining tension in the resistance band. The movement should be controlled, focusing on engaging the hamstrings and glutes. Return the leg to the extended side kick position before repeating the hook. Perform three sets of ten to twelve reps on each leg, keeping each rep deliberate and steady.

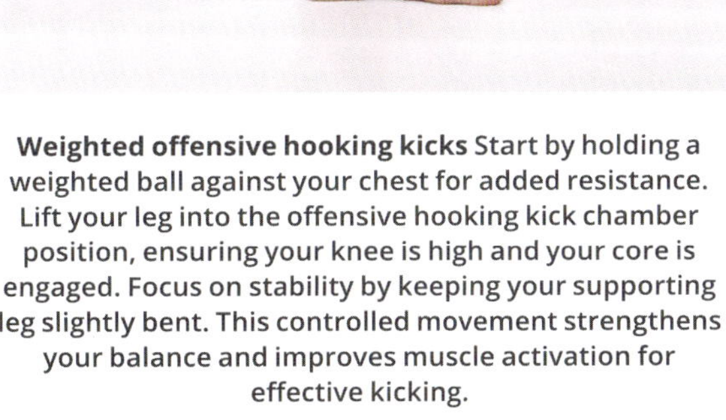

**Weighted offensive hooking kicks** Start by holding a weighted ball against your chest for added resistance. Lift your leg into the offensive hooking kick chamber position, ensuring your knee is high and your core is engaged. Focus on stability by keeping your supporting leg slightly bent. This controlled movement strengthens your balance and improves muscle activation for effective kicking.

From the hooking kick chamber, extend your leg outwards before executing a controlled hook motion back towards your body. The weighted ball adds resistance, increasing strength and power. Keep your movements slow and deliberate to avoid injury and maximise muscle engagement. Perform eight to ten repetitions on each leg for a balanced workout targeting kicking strength and flexibility.

stretches, have already been detailed to guide you through correct form and hold times. Regular practice of these stretches will help improve muscle strength, stability and flexibility, which are vital for enhancing your kicking performance. As your flexibility increases, you'll also reduce the risk of injury and achieve smoother, more powerfully executed hooking kicks. Try out the stretches shown here.

## KEY ELEMENTS COVERED IN THIS CHAPTER

- Understanding the fundamental principles of the hooking kick, including proper chambering, extension, and retraction of the kicking leg, essential for generating power and precision
- Differentiating the hooking kick from other kicks by recognising its unique mechanics

Seated static stretching is an excellent way to improve flexibility and control in your hook kick. Holding your foot in this stretch position helps loosen the hip and glute muscles, which are essential for both offensive and defensive hooking kicks. Make sure to maintain good posture and hold the stretch for 20–30 seconds for maximum benefit.

Training with a partner can enhance your passive static stretching routine. Partner-assisted stretches in a side kick position are highly beneficial for developing flexibility and strength in your hooking kick. Regular practice in this stretch will improve your range of motion and control, making both defensive and offensive hooking kicks more effective in sparring and patterns.

and applications, as well as avoiding common technical mistakes

- Recognising the importance of proper technique and alignment, including the role of the hip, knee and foot in executing the hooking kick effectively and safely
- Exploring strength and conditioning exercises tailored to target the muscle groups involved in the hooking kick, such as the hamstrings, quadriceps, gluteus maximus, core and adductors, to enhance power and stability.
- Implementing static stretching routines designed to improve flexibility and range of motion, vital for performing hooking kicks with fluidity and minimising the risk of injury

## LOOKING AHEAD

In the next chapter, we will explore inward and outward crescent kicks. These kicks introduce a new set of techniques and angles that broaden the range of striking options available to practitioners. By refining the crescent kicks, you will enhance your ability to deliver precise, curved strikes and improve your overall versatility in Taekwon-Do.

**Box split** The box split is an essential stretch for improving hip flexibility and leg mobility, crucial for effective martial arts kicking techniques. Ensure the feet are pointing forwards to properly engage the adductors and avoid unnecessary strain on the knees. Keep your hands on the floor for balance, maintain a straight back and engage your core to maximise the stretch safely.

# 13 CRESCENT KICKS

The crescent kick *(bandal chagi)*, in its two forms, the inward crescent kick *(anuro bandal chagi)* and outward crescent kick *(bakuro bandal chagi)*, is a versatile and fluid technique in Taekwon-Do. It is primarily used for blocking attacks aimed at the middle section or above while simultaneously setting up opportunities for swift counter-attacks. This kick's unique arc and dynamic execution make it invaluable in both offensive and defensive contexts.

In this chapter, we'll explore the mechanics, applications, and conditioning exercises for both the inward and outward crescent kick, with a focus on their effectiveness in sparring and self-defence.

An outward crescent kick demonstrated with height and control, arcing across the body in a wide, sweeping motion. This technique uses the instep or sole to strike or deflect, combining flexibility, fluid motion and precision. Ideal for breaking guard, redirecting attacks or targeting exposed areas.

## APPLICATION OF CRESCENT KICKS

Crescent kicks are primarily defensive techniques, designed for blocking, redirecting, or creating openings in an opponent's guard. Unlike techniques such as side kicks or turning kicks, which generate significant linear force for breaking, crescent kicks rely on a circular motion, making them less effective for direct impact-based applications such as power breaking.

Instead of breaking boards or striking with maximum force, crescent kicks excel in self-defence scenarios and sparring, where they can be used to intercept incoming attacks or disrupt an opponent's balance. In competition settings, they are often employed as a means to clear an opponent's guard before following up with a scoring technique.

Due to their specific mechanics and purpose, crescent kicks are not included in traditional power breaking disciplines. However, their versatility and fluidity make them an essential tool for Taekwon-Do practitioners seeking to refine their defensive and offensive strategies.

## MECHANICS OF THE CRESCENT KICK

A key characteristic of the crescent kick is that it allows the practitioner to maintain balance and readiness for immediate counter-attacks. For this reason, it is essential to focus on rechambering and posture throughout the motion. Proper execution requires keeping the back heel faced downward at the moment of the block, ensuring stability and alignment. The foot sole is used as the blocking tool, either the side sole or the inner sole/reverse footsword.

The crescent kick is executed in an arcing motion, with the inner sole or the footsword of the foot serving as the primary tool for blocking or striking. The trajectory is controlled and precise, reaching the target in a smooth arc to intercept or disrupt an opponent's attack.

This image highlights the striking surfaces used in crescent kicks: the inner sole for inward crescent kicks and the side sole for outward crescent kicks. Precision in foot positioning is key to effective contact, allowing the kick to sweep across the target with control, flexibility and intent.

## INWARD CRESCENT KICK

**Inward crescent kick** Begin in a strong fighting stance with both hands guarding the face. Keep your body relaxed, core engaged, and your supporting foot pointing forward. The kicking leg is slightly back, ready to initiate movement. Maintain focus on your target to ensure accuracy and control during the kick.

Chamber the kicking leg by lifting the knee to the side with a slight outward rotation. The foot should be pointed upwards, preparing for the inward sweeping motion. Keep your balance centred and your core tight. The supporting heel stays grounded, allowing for better stability and smooth execution of the technique.

At the peak of the kick, the leg creates a controlled arc, sweeping from the outside inwards. The inside edge, inner sole of the foot should be aligned with the target. Keep your upper body steady and arms in a guard position. The kicking leg moves smoothly, maintaining precision and power throughout the kick.

After the kick, retract the leg back to the chambered position to maintain balance. Ensure that the knee stays lifted momentarily before lowering the foot to the ground. Keep your hands up in guard, ready for follow-up techniques. Proper rechambering allows for faster recovery and effective transitions into subsequent movements.

The inward crescent kick can be effectively used to intercept or deflect an opponent's incoming strike. In this defensive application, the inside arc of the kick redirects the opponent's attack, particularly mid or high strikes. Ensure that the kick is well timed, aiming to disrupt the opponent's offensive momentum while maintaining your balance and guard position.

## OUTWARD CRESCENT KICK

**Outward crescent kick** Start in a fighting stance with your guard raised to protect your face. Shift your weight onto the supporting leg, allowing the kicking leg to begin its movement. The kicking leg should lift towards the opposite side, creating a smooth pathway for the outward crescent arc. Maintain a stable base and balanced posture throughout.

Lift the kicking leg across the body, with the knee bent and the foot flexed upward. The toes should point toward the ceiling to prepare for the outward swing. Ensure the hands remain in a defensive position to protect against potential counterattacks. This chambering phase sets up the kick's power, control and precision.

Extend the kicking leg outwards in a controlled arc, sweeping from one side to the other. The strike should make contact with the outer edge of the foot. Keep the movement fluid and avoid any jerking motions. The kick should be smooth, with the back foot remaining firmly grounded to maintain balance and power.

After completing the arc, quickly bring the kicking leg back across the body by bending the knee into a chambered position. Rechambering ensures balance and prepares you for follow-up techniques or defensive moves. Keep your guard up, core engaged, and return to the fighting stance. Proper rechambering helps avoid leaving yourself exposed to counter-attacks.

The outward crescent kick is highly effective for blocking or redirecting attacks, especially when combined with lateral movement. The sweeping arc using the side sole can disrupt the opponent's trajectory, create space and prevent them from closing in. Additionally, this technique can seamlessly flow into consecutive kicks or counterattacks, keeping the practitioner in control during close combat.

## USES OF CRESCENT KICKS IN SPARRING

Both inward and outward crescent kicks are versatile techniques in Taekwon-Do sparring that can be used for offensive attacks, defensive manoeuvres, and creating opportunities during a match. The kicks share common tactical advantages while offering distinct applications depending on the direction of the arc.

### Offensive Attacks

Crescent kicks are highly effective for breaking through an opponent's guard and striking unexpected targets. The inward crescent kick is particularly useful for high-target strikes, such as aiming at the head when the opponent's guard is down. Its inward arc can sweep around an opponent's arms to connect with the side or back of their head, causing them to drop their defence and creating opportunities for follow-up attacks. Similarly, the outward crescent kick can bypass an opponent's defensive stance by targeting the side of their body, midsection, or outer thigh. This kick's wide arc makes it a dual-purpose tool, able to both block incoming attacks and deliver a strike simultaneously.

### Defensive Measures

Both crescent kicks can be utilised as defensive tools to intercept or deflect incoming attacks. The inward crescent kick can redirect high strikes

**The outward crescent kick in defence** In the initial defensive step, the practitioner identifies an incoming strike and prepares to use an outward crescent kick to intercept. By lifting the leg outwards and aiming towards the attacking limb or the guard, this defensive technique creates a sweeping arc to deflect or disrupt the opponent's attack, reducing their momentum and balance.

The kick reaches its peak arc, making contact with the attacking arm or leg of the opponent. The outside edge of the foot is used to redirect the incoming strike. The sweeping motion prevents the opponent from completing their intended attack, creating an opening for a swift counter while maintaining balance and readiness.

After successfully deflecting the attack, the practitioner transitions into a counter-attack. Keeping a stable posture and focus, they deliver a punch or other attack to the opponent's open target area. This quick follow-up is essential to take advantage of the disrupted guard, ensuring control of the situation while maintaining defensive readiness.

or push back an advancing opponent, creating space and breaking their rhythm. Meanwhile, the outward crescent kick is effective for blocking low kicks or deflecting attacks aimed at the midsection. It can serve as a defensive barrier, neutralising the opponent's offensive pressure while allowing you to maintain control of the distance between you and your opponent.

### Creating Opportunities and Combinations

Crescent kicks are valuable for creating angles and setting up combination attacks. The inward crescent kick disrupts the opponent's balance and forces them to adjust their stance, opening up opportunities for follow-up techniques such as side or spin kicks. The outward crescent kick similarly creates gaps in the opponent's defence, making them vulnerable to subsequent strikes. Both kicks can change the angle of attack, forcing the opponent to react and adjust, which can be exploited for further combinations.

### Ring Control and Space Management

Crescent kicks are also useful for managing space and controlling the ring. Both the inward and outward variations can push the opponent back, preventing them from closing in and giving you time to reset or reposition. The outward crescent kick can be particularly effective in pushing the opponent towards the edge or corner of the ring, limiting their movement options and giving you a tactical advantage. By using these kicks strategically, practitioners can manage both offensive and defensive scenarios while maintaining control of the sparring space.

## COMMON MISTAKES AND INCORRECT TECHNIQUE

Crescent kicks, both inward and outward, require precise control, balance and technique to be effective. Common mistakes include overextending the arc, where swinging the leg too far reduces control, slows the kick and makes the practitioner vulnerable to counter-attacks. Improper chambering, such as starting the kick too low or failing to bend the knee adequately, disrupts the kick's smooth trajectory, while poor foot shape, like using the toes or instep instead of the correct striking tools, reduces impact and increases the risk of injury.

A flat trajectory or neglecting to rechamber the leg after the kick further diminishes balance and readiness for follow-up attacks. For inward crescent kicks, common errors include poor distancing, targeting and leaning forward excessively, which disrupt balance and limit follow-up options. Outward crescent kicks often suffer from misjudged distance, uncontrolled outward motion and improper hip engagement, reducing power, accuracy and recovery speed.

Foot shape mistakes, such as a floppy ankle, misaligned foot or bent toes, weaken the kick's effectiveness and increase injury risks. Finally, slow rechambering and failing to return to a stable stance leave practitioners off-balance and vulnerable to counter-attacks. Effective execution requires maintaining proper arc, foot positioning, hip engagement and quick recovery to maximise impact and minimise risk.

## STRENGTH AND CONDITIONING EXERCISES

Remember to do a warm-up before starting your exercises!

## Lower Body Strength Exercises

**Resistance band hip external rotation stretch** Start in a seated 90/90 position with both knees bent at 90 degrees–one in front and the other to the side. Loop a resistance band around both knees to engage the hip muscles. Keep your torso upright and place your hands on the floor for balance. This setup targets hip mobility, stability and external rotation control.

In the 90/90 position, ensure your front and back legs are bent at 90-degree angles. Loop a resistance band around your knees to add controlled resistance to the exercise. The band helps activate the external rotators of the hip, which are crucial for improving flexibility, stability and kicking power. Keep your core engaged and posture upright before starting the movement. Perform two to three sets of twelve to fifteen reps.

**Weighted leg raises and weighted crescent kicks** Boost your hip strength and kicking power with weighted leg exercises. For leg raises, stand tall with a leg weight on, lifting the leg dynamically to the front or side to target hip abductors and the gluteus medius. Perform three sets of twelve to fifteen reps per leg. For crescent kicks, balance on one leg and execute inward and outward crescent kicks in controlled arcs. This enhances hip mobility and control. Complete three sets of ten to twelve kicks in each direction for maximum benefit.

**Fire hydrant** Begin in a tabletop position with your hands directly under your shoulders and knees under your hips. Engage your core to stabilise your posture. This position sets a strong foundation for the fire hydrant exercise, targeting the hip flexors and gluteus medius. Ensure your back remains straight to prevent strain during the movement.

From the tabletop position, lift one knee out to the side, keeping it bent at a 90-degree angle. Focus on engaging the glute muscles as you lift. For added difficulty, attach ankle weights. Maintain a controlled motion to maximise activation of the hip flexors and gluteus medius. Perform three sets of ten to twelve reps on each side for best results.

# FLEXIBILITY AND MOBILITY EXERCISES

## Dynamic Stretches

**Open and close the gate** Begin by lifting your knee high in front of you, mimicking a marching movement. Keep your hands in a guard position for balance. Engage your core and stabilise the standing leg. This movement prepares your hips for more dynamic motions, increasing hip mobility and preventing injuries during kicks.

After lifting your knee, rotate it outwards in a controlled motion, as if opening a gate. Ensure your supporting leg remains stable, with your torso upright. Reverse the movement to bring the knee back to the front, closing the gate. This dynamic drill enhances hip rotation and flexibility, essential for martial arts kicking techniques. Perform one to two sets of ten reps in each direction.

**Quadriceps stretch with contract-relax wall stretch (PNF technique)** Position yourself in a kneeling stance with one leg forward and the other foot against a wall. Push your back foot into the wall to contract the quadriceps, holding the tension for a few seconds. Then release the contraction to deepen the stretch. This contract-relax method enhances flexibility by engaging and relaxing the muscle. Hold the stretch for 20–30 seconds per leg. Repeat two to three times.

## Static Stretches

**Folded forward pigeon pose** The folded forward pigeon pose stretches the hip flexors, glutes and lower back. Begin with one leg bent in front and the other extended back. Lean forward, resting your forearms on the ground to deepen the stretch. This variation promotes relaxation and increases mobility, aiding flexibility for martial arts techniques. Hold for 20–30 seconds per side.

**Block-assisted pigeon pose** This pigeon pose offers added support for those with tight hips. Place a block under your forearms to reduce tension and maintain a stable posture while folding forward. This variation allows gradual progress in flexibility by relieving pressure on the hips and promoting a more comfortable stretch. Hold for 20–30 seconds per side, focusing on steady breathing.

**Wall-elevated hamstring stretch** This stretch targets the hamstrings and improves flexibility for high kicks. Place your heel against a wall at hip height or higher, keeping your supporting leg straight. Gently lean forward to deepen the stretch without rounding your back. Maintain a slight bend in the standing leg for balance. Hold for 20–30 seconds on each side.

## KEY ELEMENTS COVERED IN THIS CHAPTER

- The strategic applications of the inward crescent kick for breaking an opponent's guard and creating openings for follow-up attacks
- The versatility of the outward crescent kick in targeting the midsection, managing distance and controlling the ring
- The dynamic offensive and defensive capabilities these kicks bring to Taekwon-Do sparring, enabling adaptability against various opponents
- The importance of precision, timing and control in executing these kicks to maximise their effectiveness in sparring scenarios

An offensive hooking kick aimed to the opponent's head, arcing around the guard with speed and precision. This technique uses the heel or sole to strike from the outside line, combining flexibility, timing and intent to deliver a sharp, unexpected blow to a high target.

# 14 EXERCISES AND WORKOUTS FOR KICKING STRENGTH AND FLEXIBILITY

Kicking strength and flexibility are fundamental to the martial artist's ability to deliver powerful, precise kicks. While strength enhances the force and control behind each strike, flexibility allows for fluidity and range of motion, enabling kicks to be executed effortlessly at varying heights and angles. This chapter explores a variety of drills and workouts specifically designed to improve kicking strength and flexibility, providing the foundation for technical mastery and optimal performance.

An advanced flying side kick captured mid-air: explosive, controlled and perfectly aligned. This high-level technique combines speed, power, and timing, using full-body momentum to deliver a forceful strike with the foot sword. A bold display of athleticism, precision and dynamic Taekwon-Do skill.

## DYNAMIC STRETCHING FOR FLEXIBILITY

Dynamic stretching is essential before any intense kicking session. It prepares the muscles, joints, and ligaments for high-impact movements, reduces the risk of injury and improves the overall range of motion. Dynamic stretching exercises should be performed before training to warm up and enhance flexibility progressively. Examples include:

- Leg swings (front and side)
- Walking lunges with a twist
- High knee pulls
- Hip circles

## STRENGTH EXERCISES FOR KICKING POWER

Building strength in the lower body is vital for delivering powerful kicks. These drills focus on increasing strength, stability, and endurance in the muscles used for kicking, particularly the hips, thighs, glutes and core.

- Squat to front kick
- Resistance band kicks
- Side leg lifts with ankle weights
- Explosive box jumps
- Pistol squats

## FLEXIBILITY EXERCISES FOR KICKING RANGE

Improving your flexibility is a continuous process that requires both dynamic and static stretching. The following flexibility exercises are designed to progressively increase your kicking height and fluidity.

- Butterfly stretch
- Pigeon pose
- Frog stretch
- Standing splits against a wall

## COOL-DOWN STRETCHES

After an intense kicking session, it's important to cool down to prevent muscle stiffness. The following stretches, plus others outlined in this book, will help with recovery and maintaining flexibility.

- Seated forward bend
- Standing quad stretch
- Supine spinal twist

## SAMPLE SHORT WORKOUTS

### Workout 1: Fundamental Kick Techniques

**Warm-up** – 2 minutes

1. Jumping jacks – 1 minute
2. Leg swings – 30 seconds each leg (front to back)

**Main workout** – 7 minutes

1. Front kick practice – 1 minute each leg
   From a fighting stance, lift your knee and snap your foot forward, aiming with the ball of your foot. Focus on proper form and control.
2. Turning kick drills – 1 minute each leg
   Pivot on your supporting foot, swing your kicking leg in a horizontal arc, striking with the shin or the instep. Emphasise hip rotation.
3. Side kick steps – 1 minute each leg
   Step behind your supporting foot, lift your knee and extend your leg sideways, pushing through the heel. Keep your body sideways to the target.
4. Back kick practice – 1 minute alternating legs
   Look over your shoulder, lift your knee, and thrust your foot backwards, hitting with the heel. Maintain balance and accuracy.

**Cool-Down** – 1 minute

1. Standing hamstring stretch – 30 seconds each leg

### Workout 2: Power and Speed Enhancement

**Warm-up** – 2 minutes

1. High knees – 1 minute
2. Butt kicks – 1 minute

**Main workout** – 7 minutes

1. Fast front kicks – 1 minute alternating legs
   Perform front kicks rapidly while maintaining good form. Aim for speed without sacrificing technique.
2. Jumping roundhouse kicks – 1 minute each leg
   Add a hop before executing the roundhouse kick to develop explosive power.
3. Back kicks – 1 minute alternating legs
   Spin on your supporting foot, locate the target over your shoulder, and execute a back kick.
4. Double kick combos – 1 minute
   Combine two kicks (for example a front kick followed by a roundhouse kick) on the same or alternating legs.
5. Burpee kickouts – 1 minute
   From a standing position, drop into a burpee, but as you come up, perform a front kick.

**Cool-down** – 1 minute

1. Quad stretch – 30 seconds each leg

### Workout 3: Flexibility and Control

**Warm-up** – 2 minutes

1. Arm circles – 30 seconds forward, 30 seconds backward
2. Hip rotations – 1 minute

**Main workout** – 7 minutes

1. Slow high front kicks – 1 minute each leg
   Execute front kicks slowly, lifting as high as possible to improve flexibility and control.
2. Chambered side kick holds – 30 seconds each leg
   Hold the side kick position with your leg extended to build strength and balance.
3. Crescent kicks – 1 minute each leg
   Swing your leg in an arc from outside to inside (outer crescent) and inside to outside (inner crescent), keeping the leg straight.
4. Axe kicks – 1 minute alternating legs
   Lift your leg straight up and bring it down forcefully with the heel toward the target.
5. shadow kicking combinations – 1 minute
   Practice various kick combinations in the air, focusing on smooth transitions and form.

**Cool-down** – 1 minute

1. Butterfly stretch – 1 minute

## FOUR-WEEK KICK STRENGTH AND FLEXIBILITY CALENDAR FOR BEGINNERS

This four-week calendar is designed to help martial artists progressively build their kicking strength and flexibility. Each week introduces new drills while reinforcing the fundamentals. Follow the plan consistently to see improvements in your kicking power, range of motion and overall flexibility. You can add the workout elements around your existing training programme, add in more elements or simply follow the programme as it is.

## Week 1: Foundations of Strength and Flexibility

Goal: Establish basic strength and flexibility while preparing the body for more intensive work in later weeks.

| Day | Focus | Workout/drills |
|---|---|---|
| **Monday** | Dynamic flexibility | Light warm-up<br>Leg swings (front and side): 3 × 10 each leg<br>High knee pulls: 3 × 10 each leg<br>Hip circles: 2 × 15 rotations each direction |
| **Tuesday** | Kicking strength | Light warm-up<br>Squat to front kick: 3 × 10 each leg<br>Side leg lifts with ankle weights: 3 × 12 each leg<br>Explosive box jumps: 3 × 10 |
| **Wednesday** | Flexibility and recovery | Butterfly stretch: 3 × 60 seconds<br>Pigeon pose: 2 × 60 seconds each leg<br>Seated forward bend: 2 × 60 seconds |
| **Thursday** | Kicking technique and mobility | Light warm-up<br>Squat to kick: 3 × 10 each leg<br>Resistance band roundhouse kicks: 3 × 12 each leg<br>Walking lunges with twist: 3 × 10 |
| **Friday** | Strength and conditioning | Light warm-up<br>Squat to side kick: 3 × 10 each leg<br>Resistance band roundhouse kicks: 3 × 12 each leg<br>Core plank hold: 3 × 60 seconds |
| **Saturday** | Flexibility and core strength | Light warm-up<br>Frog stretch: 2 × 60 seconds<br>Side split practice: 2 × 60 seconds<br>Bicycle crunches: 3 × 20 |
| **Sunday** | Active recovery | Light jog or walk: 30 minutes<br>Hip flexor stretch: 2 × 60 seconds each side<br>Hamstring stretch: 2 × 60 seconds each side |

## Week 2: Building on the Basics

Goal: Increase the intensity of strength and flexibility exercises while working on fluidity in kicks.

| Day | Focus | Workout/drills |
|---|---|---|
| **Monday** | Dynamic flexibility | Light warm-up<br>Leg swings (front and side): 3 × 12 each leg<br>Walking lunges with twist: 3 × 12<br>Hip circles: 3 × 15 rotations |
| **Tuesday** | Strength for higher kicks | Light warm-up<br>Pistol squats: 3 × 6 each leg<br>Squat to front kick: 3 × 12 each leg<br>Explosive box jumps: 3 × 12 |
| **Wednesday** | Stretching and mobility | Butterfly stretch: 3 × 60 seconds<br>Hip flexor stretch: 3 × 60 seconds each side<br>Standing splits (wall): 2 × 60 seconds |
| **Thursday** | Kicking Technique | Light warm-up<br>Squat to kicks: 3 × 12 each leg<br>Side leg lifts with ankle weights: 3 × 15 each leg<br>Resistance band roundhouse: 3 × 15 each leg |
| **Friday** | Strength and conditioning | Light warm-up<br>Squat to side kick: 3 × 12 each leg<br>Core plank hold: 4 × 60 seconds<br>Side kicks with resistance band: 3 × 12 each leg |
| **Saturday** | Flexibility focus | Pigeon pose: 3 × 60 seconds each leg<br>Seated forward bend: 2 × 60 seconds<br>Frog stretch: 3 × 60 seconds |
| **Sunday** | Active recovery | Light jog or walk: 30 minutes<br>Supine spinal twist: 3 × 60 seconds each side<br>Quadriceps stretch: 2 × 60 seconds each side |

## Week 3: Power and Range Expansion

Goal: Focus on explosive power and extending range of motion, especially for high kicks.

| Day | Focus | Workout/drills |
|---|---|---|
| **Monday** | Dynamic flexibility | Light warm-up<br>Leg swings (front and side): 3 × 15 each leg<br>High knee pulls: 3 × 12 each leg<br>Hip circles: 3 × 20 rotations |
| **Tuesday** | Strength for explosive kicks | Light warm-up<br>Pistol squats: 3 × 8 each leg<br>Explosive box jumps: 4 × 10<br>Squat to roundhouse kick: 3 × 12 each leg |
| **Wednesday** | Advanced flexibility | Light warm-up<br>Standing splits (wall): 3 × 60 seconds each leg<br>Side split practice: 3 × 60 seconds<br>Butterfly stretch: 3 × 60 seconds |
| **Thursday** | Power kicking drills | Light warm-up<br>Side leg lifts with resistance band: 4 × 15 each leg<br>Front kicks with resistance band: 3 × 12 each leg<br>Back kicks with resistance band: 3 × 12 each leg |
| **Friday** | Conditioning and core | Light warm-up<br>Side kicks with resistance band: 3 × 15 each leg<br>Core plank hold: 4 × 60 seconds<br>Bicycle crunches: 4 × 25 |
| **Saturday** | Flexibility recovery | Pigeon pose: 3 × 60 seconds each leg<br>Frog stretch: 3 × 60 seconds<br>Hip flexor stretch: 3 × 60 seconds each side |
| **Sunday** | Active recovery | Light jog or walk: 30 minutes<br>Hamstring stretch: 3 × 60 seconds each leg<br>Quadriceps stretch: 3 × 60 seconds each leg |

## Week 4: Maximising Strength and Flexibility

Goal: Integrate everything learned to achieve optimal kicking power and flexibility.

| Day | Focus | Workout/drills |
|---|---|---|
| **Monday** | Dynamic flexibility | Light warm-up<br>Leg swings (front and side): 3 × 20 each leg<br>High knee pulls: 3 × 15 each leg<br>Hip circles: 3 × 20 rotations each direction |
| **Tuesday** | Explosive strength training | Light warm-up<br>Pistol squats: 4 × 8 each leg<br>Squat to front kick: 4 × 12 each leg<br>Explosive box jumps: 4 × 12 |
| **Wednesday** | Advanced flexibility | Light warm-up<br>Standing splits (wall): 3 × 60 seconds each leg<br>Side split practice: 3 × 60 seconds<br>Butterfly stretch: 3 × 60 seconds |
| **Thursday** | Advanced kicking drills | Light warm-up<br>Weighted kicks: 4 × 12 each leg<br>Side kicks with resistance band: 4 × 15 each leg<br>Roundhouse kicks with resistance band: 4 × 12 each leg |
| **Friday** | Strength and conditioning | Light warm-up<br>Side kicks with ankle weights: 4 × 15 each leg<br>Core plank hold: 5 × 60 seconds<br>Bicycle crunches: 5 × 30 |
| **Saturday** | Flexibility and core | Pigeon pose: 3 × 60 seconds each leg<br>Frog stretch: 3 × 60 seconds<br>Supine spinal twist: 3 × 60 seconds each side |
| **Sunday** | Active recovery | Light jog or walk: 30 minutes<br>Quadriceps stretch: 3 × 60 seconds each leg<br>Seated forward bend: 3 × 60 seconds |

By the end of this four-week programme, you should feel stronger, more flexible and more confident in your kicking abilities. Continue to build on this foundation to reach even higher levels of performance!

## TIPS FOR SUCCESS

- **Consistency is key** Follow the calendar day by day, taking rest when needed, but ensure you maintain regular sessions.
- **Focus on form** As you progress through the weeks, focus on proper form for both kicks and stretches to avoid injury.
- **Listen to your body** Flexibility improves over time, but pushing too hard too soon can lead to setbacks. Be patient with your progress.
- **Adjust to your needs** Feel free to modify the repetitions or time durations to suit your current fitness level, but aim to push yourself as you progress.

A high back kick executed with precision, driven by hip rotation and spatial awareness, striking with the heel or sole. This technique delivers maximum force while keeping the body protected, showcasing balance, power and perfect timing against a rear or side-positioned opponent.

The practitioner lifts the knee high in preparation for a flying front kick, generating upward momentum, engaging the core and positioning the body for explosive elevation. This chamber is key to height, balance and control in airborne techniques.

A flying front kick in full extension, delivered with precision, elevation and striking power. Launching off the ground, the practitioner targets high with the ball of the foot, showcasing timing, athleticism and dynamic control in the air.

# Index

First published in 2025 by
The Crowood Press Ltd
Ramsbury, Marlborough
Wiltshire SN8 2HR

**enquiries@crowood.com**
**www.crowood.com**



**British Library Cataloguing-in-Publication Data**
A catalogue record for this book is available from the British Library.

For product safety-related questions please contact: productsafety@crowood.com.

**ISBN 978 0 7198 4549 9**



**Disclaimer**
The information provided in this book is intended for general knowledge and informational purposes only. It is not a substitute for professional medical advice, diagnosis or treatment. Always seek the advice of your doctor or other qualified healthcare provider before starting any new exercise, fitness, or dietary programme.

Performing the exercises or utilising any information in this book is at your own risk. Neither the author nor the publisher shall be held liable for any injuries, health issues or damages resulting from the use of this book. By using this book, you agree to assume full responsibility for any and all injuries or damages that may occur, and you expressly waive any claims against the author or publisher arising from your use of the information or exercises contained herein.

Typeset by Simon and Sons

Cover design by Samantha Rolfe-Hoang

Printed and bound in India by Thomson Press India Ltd

## ACKNOWLEDGEMENTS

This book would not have been possible without the unwavering support of those who have been part of my Taekwon-Do journey.

To my students – your trust and dedication inspire me to grow as a coach and continually strive for improvement. To my fellow coaches and mentors – your wisdom and shared experiences have shaped my technical understanding and coaching philosophy.

To my husband, family, friends, and the parents of my students – your belief in me has been a constant source of encouragement. Thank you for your constant support and encouragement.

This book is a testament to the power of community, perseverance, and the love of Taekwon-Do. Thank you to everyone who has been part of this journey.

Photography by Pieter Uys

Athletes: Sally Gleaves, Adam Monks and Amy Pullen

# ALSO BY THE AUTHOR

Increased Conditioning, Mobility and Flexibility

태권도 발차기

## ADVANCED TAEKWON-DO KICKS

Blue to Black Belt

**Sally Gleaves**

6th Degree ITF Taekwon-Do

# RELATED TITLES